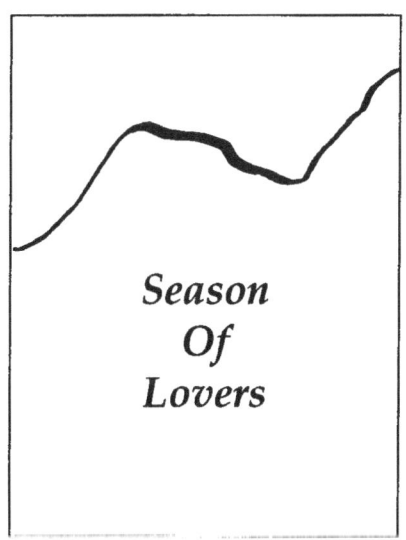

Season
Of
Lovers

Readers Comment ~

"Mary Carol Lewis has given an authentic voice to the single life. Her willingness to search honestly, remain open and find hope are written on every page. You witness and experience the coming into the fullness of the self. A tribute to a life of all kinds of loving."
— Ginger Sullivan Schneider, MA, LPC, CGP

"It evoked in me a bigger sense of my own humanity and the enjoyment of life and gratitude for the subtlety and gentleness of my own inner and outer experiences in living. Thanks for being transparent enough to allow others to read your thoughts in verse!"
— Kristi Maddox

"I applaud you for your efforts in addressing the needs of single adults. Keep up the good work. Congratulations. The more the merrier." — Terry Hershey, author of the best-selling book, *Beginning Again* and *Intimacy*

"Your thoughtful book, *Season of Lovers*... expresses the feelings of other singles. I pray that writing those words also brought you pleasure and peace." —Lucy Marsden-Hottle

"*Season of Lovers* tells us that relationships change like the seasons, and that we must change: by becoming more forgiving, discovering that we can trust God, and coming to know ourselves more completely." — Jim Ellingsworth

"A thoroughly enjoyable and vivid reminder of the restorative power of nature, the freedom of imagination, and the eloquence of the written word." — Jim Chamberlin

Season
of
Lovers

A Seasonal Journey
Toward Sensual Refreshment

from the journal images of
Mary Carol Lewis

With original artwork by Cathryn Stephens

Published by
Singles Network Press
PO Box 13
Springfield, VA 22150-0013

www.Network4Singles.com

Original artwork by
Cathryn Stephens © 2000

Ms Stephens is a freelance artist
working in northern Virginia.

Mary Carol Lewis is the penname of a freelance writer in Northern
Virginia whose pieces have appeared often in the *Singles Network
Newsletter,* www.Network4Singles.com and trade magazines.
Her work has inspired individuals toward personal growth for many
years. The images in this volume were selected from her personal
journal and photographic collections over the past six years.

To My Beloved:

Waiting for *true love* to capture you
   and hold you close,
Creating yourself anew
   so that you can live graciously
   in relationship with someone
   who opens the inner heart to your love,
You are still a sensuous person.
All your senses are alive –
And keeping all your senses alive and well
   is the challenge that is set before you.
Alone time is a season full of
tempestuous storms and quiet reverie.
These are images from my sojourn
   in that season.
May they bless you in your journey.

Thanks, Jack, for letting me use your name.

And a special thanks
To those dearest to my heart –
   You know who you are.♥

Table of Contents

Section	Page

Section	Page

"Nature never deserts the wise and pure,
No plot so narrow, be but nature there;
No waste so vacant, but may well employ
*   each faculty of sense,*
And keep the heart awake to love and beauty!"
— Coleridge

List of Quotations
Verses from the following selections appear in this volume

"To see a World in a grain of sand,
And a Heaven in a wild flower;
Hold Infinity in the palm of your hand,
And Eternity in an hour."
— William Blake

During my alone time
I have had many lovers:
Among them the mountains,
The streamside, the sea.
There were many surprise meetings
And gentle moments,
Joyous pleasures and
Soft reverie with someone special.
But always, always
There was the gracious love
Of the One who created
The beauty that surrounds me,
The One who knows me best.
So that all in all, I know
That truly, truly
I am loved.
Thank you for calling me your *Beloved.*

"A woman can be both moral and exciting
So long as she makes it look like quite a struggle."
— Edna Ferber

Sunlight and Shadows

Brother of the Sun

O, Brother of the Sun, Come!
Warm me with your sweet caress
That enters my very being
And brings a welcome spring
To all that lies in winter dormancy within.

My spirit longs for your spirit.
Come, thou long-awaited one.
Bring with you the music
That brings a symphony to my inner chamber,
And cleanse my body with the waters
   that flow only from you.

Touch my body with the spirit of the Earth
Which you represent in my presence.
Teach me the rhythm of the Cosmos
   from which you spring:
The constancy of the stars,
The radiance of the full moon,
The mysterious *otherness* of dark,
   billowing clouds gathering for a tempest.
The majestic spirit of the thunder,
The gentle refreshment of the rain,
The slow, quiet opening of a blossom,
The bidding of the tiny sparrow
Who lacks the feathers (and the desire)
   to leave the nest.
The powerful, cascading river
That moves everything in its path
   to new adventures,
The ebb and flow of the waves of the sea,
The gentle comfort that settles in the garden
As the last raindrops fall quiet from the trees.

Touch me soft with your caresses.
Gentle my senses with your smooth hand
Moving along my body like the sun on a dial –
As the long minutes pass,
Over and over as the spring rains
That seem to follow one another
As endlessly as the seasons follow:
Follow, follow, never catching up
But *never* dropping off.
Bringing hope that you will never, *never* stop –
Except, perhaps, in ecstasy.

You draw me to your warm succulence
And soothe my fears with a touch.
Your touch draws a whimper from me:
Anxiety that my very clothing
Excludes you from my warmth.
I long to open myself to your embrace.

You move around me:
Softly and slowly as the newborn pup
That nuzzles his mother's body
    for the warm milk
That sustains his life and brings joy to his soul,
Caressing and playful as a melody
That soothes and capers
Around my head and body
When music is playing.
Sing to me, Brother of the Sun.

Your hand strokes,
And your body presents itself manly before me
And your kisses seek
And give reassurance that all is well.
I feel all of security within your arms.

You speak softly and slowly,
But not as slowly as your hand,
Which speaks a language
    that my body understands.
My body knows the sweetness and glory
Of the language your hand whispers to it.
And it responds – slowly at first
Like a waking child,
Then ever more warmly and spontaneously.
My body recognizes you.
There are beautiful melodies dancing in my head
And lovely scenes
Shimmering in my eye's darkness as you kiss,
And there is ecstasy rising and greeting you,
Brother of the Sun.

And as you continue to caress my body
And explore my soul –
Your fingers and lips begin their search
Of the lesser known regions.
Your touch finds its way
To the secret places of my body
And whisper again to my soul.

And the melody which you strum upon my body
Finds an echoing chord in yours
And my hand soothes away your concerns
And caresses your soul.

You pass your fingers deftly through my hair –
Rejoicing in the soft curls.
My hand works its way through your hair –
Caressing and compelling.
My touch is careless but deliberate,
Slow but stimulating –
It begins to waft within your soul
Toward your secret places.

Your touch falls gently upon my breast
And the wonder in your face
Shows your pleasure with its smooth roundness.
My nipples rouse slowly and touch your fingers
With their firmness.
They long for your lips.
O Brother of the Sun,
Rise upon me and fill me
    with your fruitful warmth.

Ah, the memory is strong,
The images are sweet,
The love is wholesome,
But the chamber is empty,
And so I wait.

Come and drive away the muffled chill of winter
That lies deep within me.
Come and bring summer to my body
And joy to my soul. Come.
I am waiting for you.

"Let him kiss me with the kisses of his mouth;
for thy love is better than wine.
Because of the savor of thy good ointments
Thy name is as ointment poured forth,
Therefore do the virgins love thee...
Thy cheeks are comely with rows of jewels,
Thy neck with chains of gold...
A bundle of myrrh is my well-beloved to me;
He shall lie all night between my breasts.
My beloved is to me as a cluster of cypress
in the vineyards of Engedi.
Behold, thou art fair, my love.
Behold, thou art fair;
Thou hast dove's eyes.
Behold thou are fair, my beloved,
Yea, pleasant, also our bed is green.
The beams of our house are cedar,
And our rafters of fir.
Song of Solomon 1:2-10

"The moth's kiss, first!
Kiss me as if you made believe
You were not sure, this eve,
How my face, your flower, had pursed
Its petals up; so, here and there
You brush it, till I grow aware
Who wants me, and wide ope I burst.

The bee's kiss, now!
Kiss me as if you entered gay
My heart at some noonday,
A bud that dares not disallow
The claim, so all is rendered up,
And passively its shattered cup
Over your head to sleep I bow.
　　　　　—Robert Browning

"Thy song, Lark, is strong;...
There is madness about thee, and joy divine
In that song of thine; ...
Joyous as morning,
Thou art laughing and scorning;
Thou hast a nest for thy love and thy rest,...
With a soul as strong as a mountain river
Pouring out praise to the almighty Giver,
    Joy and jollity be with us both!
Alas! My journey, rugged and uneven,
Through prickly moors or dusty ways must wind;
But hearing thee, or others of thy kind,
    As full of gladness and as free of heaven,
I, with my fate contented, will plod on,
And hope for higher raptures,
    When life's day is done."

      from "To a Skylark"
      — William Wordsworth (1805)

The Century's Last Eclipse

There are signs in the heavens,
 and this partially eclipsed sunrise is no exception.
I do not know what I will discover about my world,
 but I made my plans carefully last night
 and ventured onto the hillside behind my house
 around five am on this morning of the eclipse.
The sky is clear from one horizon to the other
 and Cassiopeia is at the zenith
 with the North Star and Venus not far away.
The big dipper has already set, Orion is below the horizon,
 and I know where the moon is. I chuckle to myself.
It is very dark in this pre-dawn hour and an old hymn
 comes to my mind:
"And the darkness shall turn to dawning,
 and the dawning to noonday bright.
And God's great kingdom shall come on earth:
 the kingdom of love and light."
And then I begin to perceive the message for me in this
dawning.
The world about me is silent
 except for the buzzing of a few summer insects.
I can make out the sandy colored path amid the dark grasses.
The sky is a slate gray.
I had hoped that the sun would rise at the low point
 of the valley to my right.
If it did, I would be able to see the partial eclipse.
But if it rises from behind the trees,
 the eclipse will be over before it clears my horizon.
I scan the horizon anxiously, but am disappointed to discover
 a lighter section just to the left
 of the low point behind the forested area.
I watch that spot and feel – rather than see – the dawn delayed.
At first there is a shadow of a pink glaze on the tree tops –
 a pale sheen. Then the color disappears for a breathless time,
 and the world seems to wait in suspense.
There seems to be something important happening
Behind the scenes before we watchers can enjoy the sunrise.

All of nature waits with me
    while my mind wanders into reverie.
Never before did I realize how much I want the sun to rise.
Never before did I realize
    how much I take this daily miracle for granted.
I rarely appreciate this magnificent *Being* in the sky
    that comes to visit the earthbound ones
    and brings his glorious radiance to light our lives.
The sun rises on our world everyday,
    and we don't even think about the beauty it brings
    to our bodies and our souls. And now it is delayed –
    and we earth creatures are waiting anxiously.
The birds are still silent, except for an "accidental" squawk.
They are fifteen minutes behind their regular morning song.
At last the horizon grows lighter – just a pale gray-white,
And a bird in a tree somewhere sees the soft change in light
    and begins to sing.
I wish that I could be in the top of that tree with the bird.
What a spectacle I would behold.
The other birds – relieved – begin to sing on cue,
    and nature seems to relax, sigh with relief,
    and begin functioning normally again.
A few dingy bats flap here and there,
    and some gnats settle on a weed stalk –
    which has now become clearly visible.
Peace creeps into my heart slowly, imperceptibly,
    as light creeps into this pre-dawn wilderness.
"It is complete,"
I seem to hear the presence in all earthly matters assure me.
"The sun will continue its journey.
It is the dawning of a new day."
I know that the darkness I feel in my life is about to end.
Dawn is coming.
I can wait patiently for the new day to begin.

"Now air is hushed, save where the weak-eyed bat
With short, shrill shriek, flits by on leathern wing;
Or where the beetle winds
His small but sullen horn,
As of the rises 'midst the twilight path."
  — William Collins

"There is a signature of wisdom and power
impressed on the works of God,
which evidently distinguishes them
from the feeble imitations of men—
Not only the splendor of the sun,
but the glimmering light of the glowworm,
proclaims his glory."
  — John Newton

Nature Lovers

I am like a waterfall,
Magic, effervescent, unbounded and free,
Cascading wildly down the side of a mountain
That understands the capriciousness of time.
Endlessly caressing the one I call my lover.
Our bond is secure – secure and everchanging,
Fresh as the new buds of spring.

Mountain majesty, my lover,
Standing in royal splendor over the plain
Veiled in clouds and mystery
Producing vibrant new growth
From things deeply rooted within,
Holding jeweled treasures in your inner heart:
Beauty, challenge, otherness, hope.
Hold me in your arms.
Shelter me in your mystery.

So is a man who commands my attention.
Rugged masterpiece of the creator,
Mysteriously other, charmingly alluring,
Massive, challenging,
Sparkling with newness and adventure,
Solid standing with roots beyond the ancient.

And as I flow, gently stroking the land
That brings beauty and joy to my soul,
I empty myself into the ocean.
The sea that embraces me with
Its constancy, its power,
Its strength and excitement.

As I, a loving creation, sit upon the seashore
Listening to my lover call to me through the mists,
Feeling the tiny beckoning waves curling around my feet,
Drawing me toward my love. I hope in him.
Like unto the ocean is the man of my dreams,
Ever sweeping around me with his encompassing care.
Such are the depths of love.

"Bright Flower! whose home is everywhere,
Bold in maternal Nature's care...
There abides in thee
Some concord with humanity,
Given to no other flower I see
*   The forest through! ...*
Thou would teach man how to find
A shelter under every wind,
A hope for times that are unkind
*   And every season?*
Thou wander'st the wide world about
Unchecked by pride or scrupulous doubt,
With friends to greet thee, or without,
*   Yet pleased and willing;*
Meek, yielding to the occasion's call,
And all things suffering from all,
Thy function apostolical
*   In peace fulfilling."*

                    from "To the Daisy"
                    — William Wordsworth (1802)

12

Sensuous

I think of the marvelous shiny smoothness of my car
   after bathing and buffing to polished splendor,
The smell of fresh-turned earth
   when I've spent a day in the garden,
The "song" of the frogs on the evening
   before a cold front invades their watery community,
The poised neatness of the stack of papers
   for the project – completed at last,
The melting taste of meatloaf
   served in the kitchen by someone in love,
The sensuous movement of a pet,
The radiant face of the person
   receiving the bouquet the giver smelled on the sly.
Ol' Noah (the lexicographer,
   not the one with the sailing zoo)
   was right when he wrote that sensuous
   is a word meaning "pertaining to the senses."

I find favorites in the glorious multiplicity of gifts
   and joys that please the senses:
A bunch of late summer wild flowers or a gift
   from the garden – or road-side stand –
A walk in the woods, or the country, or on the seashore,
   or in the mountains or even in the neighborhood
Provides a wealth of surprises and delights:
The neighbor's new delphinium,
The tiny red bits on a woodland moss in full "bloom,"
A mockingbird singing its *joi de vivre* to the sky,
A curious cow protecting her stringy calf,
The endless roar of the ocean,
The feel of the wind in my hair,
The cool retreat into shelter,
The ecstasy of an eternity of time
   on a cliff overlooking darkening beauty –
What better gifts than these?

Children understand simple sensuousness.
They revel in the mystery of a shampoo's lather
   on their dirty scalp;
They will spend hours watching a caterpillar
   go about its business in the neighbor's tree;
They listen for the changing sound of a passing train;
They savor the delight of ice cream on a summer day;
They are alert to the smell of the ozone before a thunderstorm.

When I come through the sensuous door,
I become like a little child and share in their delights.
I enjoy being with people who enjoy weather:
Not just "good weather" but each of the numerous kinds
   of weather: misty rain, violent storms, gusty winds,
   quiet twilight, clear brightness, and on and on.

I like to lie in the grass and watch the trees blow,
Wash someone else's hair – then dive into the lake for a rinse.
Get thoroughly wet outdoors,
Pick up a pretty stone in a stream.
Ahh.   Delight!
Anyone who ignores the sensuous side of my nature
   does so at his own peril.

I began as a child
   picking up dropped blossoms in the spring
   and radiant leaves in the autumn.
I have two maple leaves mottled with scarlet and gold
   pegged to my desk wall right now.
I remember the violently beautiful day I found them last October.
February is not long enough for all the Valentines
I have to give and receive, but I find heart-shaped
"Valentines" everywhere I go, month after month:
A brilliant crimson leaf in the fall;
A smooth, white, rounded stone
   from the stream I visit on holidays;
A crooked tree limb appearing to meet the shore of a lake –
   just beside the cut of a tiny stream.
The world is full of Valentines, and I enjoy them all!

"These I have loved:
White plates and cups, clean-gleaming,
Ringed with blue lines; and feathery, faery dust;
Wet roots, beneath the lamp-light; the strong crust
Of friendly bread; and many-tasting food;
Rainbows and the blue bitter smoke of wood;
And radiant raindrops couching in cool flowers;
And flowers themselves, that sway through sunny hours,
Dreaming of moths that drink them under the moon;
Then, the cool kindliness of sheets, that soon
Smooth away trouble; and the rough male kiss
Of blankets; grainy wood; live hair that is
Shining and free; blue massing clouds; the keen
Unpassioned beauty of a great machine;
The benison of hot water; furs to touch;
The good smell of old clothes; and others such—
The comfortable smell of friendly fingers,
Hair's fragrance, and the musty reek that lingers
About dead leaves and last year's ferns...
Dear names,
And a thousand throng to me! Royal flames;
Sweet water's dimpling laugh from tap or spring;
Holes in the ground; and voices that do sing;
Voices in laughter, too; and body's pain,
Soon turned to peace; and the deep-panting train;
Firm sands; the little dulling edge of foam
That browns and dwindles as the wave goes home;
And washen stones, gay for an hour; the cold
Braveness of iron; moist black earthen mould;
Sleep; and high places; footprints in the dew;
And oaks; and brown horse-chestnuts, glossy-new;
And new-peeled sticks; and shiny pools on grass;
All these have been my love. And these shall pass, ...
Oh, never a doubt but, somewhere, I shall wake,
And give what's left of love again, and make
New friends, now strangers..."
from 'The Great Lover"
— Rupert Brooke (1915)

"The heavens declare the glory of God,
   and the firmament shows forth his handiwork.
Day unto day utters speech,
And night unto night shows knowledge.
There is no speech or language
   where their voice is not heard.
Their line is gone out through all the earth.
In them hath he set a tabernacle for the Sun,
Which is the bridegroom
Coming out of his chamber,
And rejoices as a strong man to run a race.
His going forth is from the end of the heaven,
And his circuit unto the ends of it:
And there is nothing hid from the heat thereof."
Psalm 19: 1-6

Sunlight

My kitten likes to sleep in the sunlight.
Even in late June he finds a board in the garden
    which is splattered by some cedar chips.
He plays for a while, and then he winds himself up
    and stretches himself out again.
He purrs for a while, then he sleeps in the sunlight.
He does not care about the news.
He is not concerned
    about all that is happening under the Sun.
He is not thinking about the meaning of life.
He is simply enjoying the warmth of the sun.

My children enjoy playing in the sun.
They spend long days enjoying its brightness
    and the shadows it creates for cooling off.
They shout for joy as they run and play on the grass
    it draws out of the cold, silent earth each spring.
They are not interested in information on sunlight.
They have no desire to know about photons
    and neutrons and light particles and pulsars.
They do not seek lessons on how worship of the sun
    has affected human history.
They just want to play in the sunlight.

My heart rejoices in the sunlight.
My heart welcomes each bright new day
    (each one fresher than the day before)
With songs in the garden.
I notice that the garden flowers lift their heads
    and open their beauty to receive its radiance.
They rejoice with me and sing their silent joy.
I am not concerned about the allegories
    the sun brings to mind
    as it affects our experience of life.
I'll just go outside and sing in the sunlight.

Earth has not anything to show more fair:
Dull would he be of soul who could pass by
A sight so touching in its majesty:
This City now doth like a garment wear
The beauty of the morning; silent, bare
Ships, towers, domes, theaters, and temples lie
Open unto the fields, and to the sky;
All bright and glittering in the smokeless air.
Never did sun more beautifully steep
In his first splendor valley, rock, or hill;
Ne'er saw I, never felt, a calm so deep!
The river glideth at his own sweet will:
Dear God! The very houses seem asleep;
And all that mighty heart is lying still!

Composed on Westminster Bridge
— William Wordsworth (1802)

M E M O

Dear One,

I just want you to know that I love you dearly even
though I leave you for long hours every day and spray you with
water each and every time you jump up on the dining table. (I
noticed, by the way, that you pummeled the spray bottle
yesterday when it wasn't doing anything at all, and you
threatened it within an inch of its life. But I remain undaunted:
I know it is on my side and not susceptible to your threats!)

You have helped me solve problems I was acutely
aware of and problems I still haven't identified. I was worried
that my potted plants might take over the household, so active in
propagating were they. But you have single-handedly solved
that problem. You have knocked all of them off the window sill,
one-by-one, since they were obviously distracting me from my
primary concern [you]. And the one little plant that you
identified as having positive mouse-like tendencies – especially
the broad leaves that look and feel like mouse ears between your
teeth — well, when you ran off with it dangling from your
mouth, I knew that my problem with the proliferation of plants
was at a standstill.

You have also solved my problem with how to occupy
myself at 5 am (I don't even need to set the alarm for 6 am –
unless I want to hear the news and weather). While I am
sleeping soundly – even before I wake up with the nagging
question, "What to do? What to do?" you have solved it for me.

My earlobe calls back your memory of the comfort of
your mother's milk (perhaps the hair around it is the giveaway).
And you nestle beside my head sucking and kneading in your
reverie. The obvious solution to my (previously unknown)
dilemma is to go downstairs and open a can of cat food for you.
[You seem to anticipate my every need.]

19

You have joggled my memory about the physical and emotional need to run and play. You sprint down the steps when you think I am going to open the door onto the patio and let you out into the sunlight. You chase butterflies and stage violent matches with the logs and branches whom you consider worthy opponents. You race, roll on your back and flail your legs, bat your paws, spring on everything that moves (including my foot, ouch!) You are not yet familiar with the term "velvet your claws." You have awakened me to the need and joy of child-like exercise. And after exerting yourself for hours, you curl up in a place you have taken for yourself and purr yourself gently to sleep. You have reminded me of my childhood delight in naptime.

But best of all you have taught me my need for cuddling and close companionship. Sure, I have lots of men in my life, but no-one curls himself within my arms and places his head on the crook of my arm, looks at me adoringly, and murmurs gently how he loves me like you do. Altogether we are one, we two.

"Now fades the glimmering landscape on the sight,
And all the air a solemn stillness holds,
Save where the beetle wheels his droning flight,
And drowsy tinklings lull the distant folds;
Save that from yonder ivy-mantled tower
The moping owl does to the moon complain
Of such as, wandering near her secret bower,
Molest her ancient solitary reign."
— Thomas Gray

"The whole earth is at rest and is quiet. They break forth into singing. Yes, the fir trees rejoice at thee and the cedars of Lebanon, saying, No feller is come up against us." Isaiah 14:7-8

"Wee, modest, crimson-tipped flow'r,
Thou's met me in an evil hour;
For I maun crush amang the stoure
      Thy slender stem:
To spare thee now is past my pow'r,
      Thou bonie gem.
Alas! It's no thy neebor sweet,
The bonie lark, companion meet,
Bending thee 'mang the dewy weet,
      Wi' spreckled breast!
When upward-springing, blythe, to greet
      The purpling east. ...
Thou, beneath the random bield
      O' clod or stane,
Adorns the histie stibble-field,
      Unseen, alane.
There, in thy scanty mantle clad,
Thy snawie bosom sunward spread,
Thou lifts thy unassuming head
      In humble guise;
But now the share uptears thy bed,
      And low thou lies!"

from "To a Mountain Daisy"
on turning one down with a plow April, 1786
    — Robert Burns (1786)

"Through primrose tufts, in that green bower,
The periwinkle trailed its wreaths;
And 'tis my faith that every flower
Enjoys the air it breathes."
    — William Wordsworth (1798)

Dawn on the Seashore

Hawaiian Surprise

Loneliness
Surrounded by beauty,
Heart breaking
Loveliness
That captures the soul
And holds it hostage,
And pummels it
With fragrant flowers,
And gentleness of spirit,
Brilliant sunlight,
And a flashing sea.

*"For you shall go out with joy,
and be led forth with peace;
the mountains and the hills
shall break forth before you
into singing,
and all the trees of the field
shall clap their hands."*
Isaiah 55:12

Encounter with Joy

"The secret waits for eyes unclouded by longing."
Tao Te Ching

Three times I have been surprised
As I walked along life's path
By a person who brought me an unexpected, secret joy.
Each experience brought something into my life
That I shall never forget.
I shall live forever in the radiance of those events
   of serendipitous hope.
I never expected these marvelous moments in time,
But was caught unawares just being the person that I am.
I was not expecting them, but my heart was long prepared,
And someone was watching over me.
In the summer which ended my long marriage
I met a man on Wakiki Beach. And from that time
I began to understand true intimacy.

It was early dawn, and the sun was just beginning
   to show itself in the southern sky on a cloudless day.
The hotels on the beach began to glow – one by one –
   as the sun rounded Diamond Head,
And they began to reflect its radiance.
I was on the beach early that morning –
But not as early as several other seekers:
A couple who had nestled on the beach
In yesterday's darkness – and were rousing themselves
To the experience of this new day –
Lay near my feet.
A man sat alone on a bench like mine,
And he also had his Bible open on his lap – seeking
   wisdom as I did at this new dawning in this strange land.
I did not wish to disturb his time of quiet,
But as he moved to leave the beach, I spoke to him.
He did not speak very much English,
And I speak no Korean, but within minutes
We discovered that, despite our differences,

We both listened to our Father,
So we felt ourselves to be closer than kin.
We basked together in God's radiance.
He spoke of waiting at the beach for insight and
Experiencing recovery from the blindness of constant busyness.
I listened, absorbed in the pleasure of discovering a companion
    with whom I could share my deepest thoughts. After a time
Of chatting in our halting, happy way, he said, "Pray!"
I did not understand him, but without another word
He grabbed my hand and began praying for me in Korean.
I was thrilled. He was clearly a man of God,
And I had never before been prayed for in *Korean*.
I had only known this man for five minutes,
And yet there were no barriers to the love between us:
At last I understood true intimacy.
We parted, and I went to collect my son for our walk to breakfast.
The plumaria trees had dropped several blossoms
The night before, and I placed them in my hair
As we walked along – breathing in the mysterious perfume
    of their presence.
And when we entered the restaurant
    where we breakfasted every morning – there he was!
The pastor of the church that was hosting his visit was with him,
And he told me more about this man who had brought
    so much unexpected joy into my life.
He was a Korean minister who had brought his children's choir
    to America for a tour.
Honolulu was his last stop. He had two children,
But had lost "the mother" only a few months earlier.
Of all the people in America that he had seen,
I was the only one who greeted him.
I had been on the beach that dawn for a reason –
Just as surely as he had.

   *"I thought that 'grown' was born today, but I found that
each new day is a new beginning, full of promise and
asking for a chance to express itself fully."*

"Bending beneath our life's mysterious weight
Of pain, and doubt, and fear, yet yielding not
In happiness to the happiest upon earth.
Simplicity in habit, truth in speech,
Be these the daily strengtheners of their minds;
May books and nature be their early joy?
And knowledge, rightly honored with that name—
Knowledge not purchased by the loss of power!"
      — William Wordsworth

"Whom shall teach knowledge?
And whom shall be made to understand doctrine?
Them that are weaned from the milk,
And drawn from the breasts.
For precept must be upon precept,
Precept upon precept.
Line upon line, line upon line.
Here a little, and there a little...
This is the rest by which the weary people can rest;
And this is the refreshing."
Isaiah 28: 9-10, 12

"Have you not heard that the everlasting God,
The Lord, the Creator of the ends of the earth,
Faints not, neither is weary?
There is no searching of his understanding.
He gives power to the faint,
And to them that have no might,
He increases strength.
Even the youths shall faint and be weary,
And the young men shall utterly fall.
But they that wait on the Lord
Shall renew their strength;
They shall mount up with wings like eagles.
They shall run and not be weary,
And they shall walk and not faint."
      Isaiah 40:28-31

Woods in Summer

I am alone – and yet not alone.
I hear no voices, but the sleepy birds in nearby trees
And a watchful dog in the distance
Are making their small noises.
The summer crickets surround me with their whir,
And some animal provides a cadence to the snare.
The insects move about quietly on the rocks and leaves
Without making a sound – yet they are all around.
A shaft of sunlight breaks through the open woods
And lights a stone –
As if it were the *Stone of Destiny*.
What is my destiny, I wonder?
If I knew my destiny, how would it change my life?
The low stream water sweeps around the mossy rocks
Softly, gently – hardly making a sound.
The summer drought has softened its voice,
But can never silence it.
Hands full of berries are ripe for the picking –
They shine black and beautiful
On the tips of their stems.
Many push forward
Practically thrusting themselves at the picker –
Many are only found behind
And under the sheltering leaves,
And they are the most luscious.

"Beauty within itself should not be wasted.
Fair flowers that are not gathered in their prime
Rot and consume themselves in little time."
— William Shakespeare

"Yet gleaning grapes shall be left in it, as the shaking
of an olive tree, two or three berries in the top
of the upmost bough, four or five
in the outmost fruitful branches."
Isaiah 17:6

Summer Visit

The call of the stream was loud
As I made my way down the steep hill
Seeking shelter from the sun
Beside the raucous cascade.

But I was slowed in my descent
By the berry bushes
Lying prostrate on the stony ground
With their pudgy little berries lifted,
Begging to be picked up.

Tiny hoof prints in the wet sand path
And partings in the grass
Showed that fawns had drunk clear water
Where I sat long, drinking of nature's grace.

But the sinking sun
  (and a wood tick on my blouse)
Reminded me that I must
Make my way back up the path
And return to civilization.

Fair

for his birthday ~

"Fair as a star when only one
   is shining in the sky."
Fair is the moon reigning o'er the heavens
   and blessing all beneath.
Fair is the white breast of the beach
   covered ever and anon as with a garment
   by the gentle waves of the evening sea.
And fair are my thoughts of you, *Beloved,*
As I cradle you softly in my heart.

"Near the pavilions where we slept, still ran
Soft-tinkling streams, and dashing waters fell,
And sobbing breezes sighed, and oft began
(So worked the wizard) wintry storms to swell,
As heaven and earth they would together mell;
At doors and windows, threatening, seemed to call
The demons of the tempest, growling fell;
Yet the least entrance found they none at all;
Whence sweeter grew our sleep, secure in massy hall."
   — James Thomson

"Thou art to me but as a wave
Of the wild sea; and I would have
Some claim upon thee, if I could
Though but of common neighborhood.
What joy to hear thee, and to see!"
   — William Wordsworth

Pensive Thoughts

As I open the old study books,
I find that I have not spent enough time in poetry.
Poetry, that soothes the soul
   like a matron soothes a softly sobbing child;
Poetry, that challenges the wit
   and the perception of reality;
Poetry, that reminds one of the memory fetched
   and held long ago,
Or opens the heart to things previously unseen.

Looking north, I see a pale pink rainbow lighted
   against a misty blue morning sky.
What is God's purpose in creating such stunning beauty?
Why does my heart beat so joyfully?
Why do I pose empty questions that go unanswered?
What is truly beautiful about my Self?

"When all at once I saw a crowd,
A host, of golden daffodils;
Beside the lake, beneath the trees,
Fluttering and dancing in the breeze....
The waves beside them danced; but they
Outdid the sparkling waves in glee:
A poet could not but be gay,
In such a jocund company:
I gazed—and gazed—but little thought
What wealth the show to me had brought:
For oft, when on my couch I lie
In vacant or in pensive mood,
They flash upon that inward eye
Which is the bliss of solitude;
And then my heart with pleasure fills,
And dances with the daffodils."
                    —William Wordsworth

*"In nature, things move violently to their place,
And calmly in their place."*
— Francis Bacon

*"Natural objects themselves, even when they make no claim to
beauty, excite the feelings, and occupy the imagination. Nature
pleases, attracts, delights, merely because it is nature. We
recognize in it an Infinite Power."*
— W. Humboldt

*"Nature does not capriciously scatter her secrets as golden gifts
to lazy pets and luxurious darlings, but imposes tasks when she
presents opportunities, and uplifts him whom she would inform.
The apple that she drops at the feet of Newton is but a coy
invitation to follow her to the stars."*
— E. P. Whipple

Summer Storm:
Not a Moment Too Soon

I spent only moments
By the streamside in my secret place,
But those moments deep within the forest
In the place that holds my heart
Kept me from the knowledge
That the rolling gray clouds and frisked trees –
Dancing wildly in the gusts –
Had grown into a full-blown storm
Flying from the west toward my sanctum.

When I reached the top of the hill at the edge of the forest,
The beautiful mosaic of varying tones of gray
Which hurried eastward overhead
Made it clear that there was turbulence in the heavens.
The color of the landscape had changed just as suddenly,
And the summer storm was upon me!
I had left the streamside not a moment too soon.

The wind played at my back,
Combed the weeds and buffeted the trees
As I raced home through the grassland ahead of the storm.
Thunder rumbled in the distance and a few drops of rain
Indicated the storm's full intent.
I was not afraid of a soaking – I'm wash and wear –
But I realized as I climbed up and down
The hills of grassy fields toward home
That I was the tallest created thing in the area,
And though I had not yet seen a flash,
The thunder gave the warning.
I met children dancing in the different feel of the weather
And watched the sheets of gray rain
Cut me off from the forest.
The storm soon passed – as these storms do –
And peace wandered aimlessly about the land.

Wind in the Mountains

Surprise

I had hoped to have a lover near me
When I walked the path of pain
But I discover that few are willing
To take that walk with me.

Sunny has gone behind a cloud
Of his own painful memories
About a lost wife who faced surgery
And debilitation and death.
The brown mouse has become frightened
And withdrawn behind his peephole,
And the otter seeks peace
   upon another shore,
Where he is mourning another loss,
As I face a danger
I have thought of
Only in my wildest dreams.

I seem to be all alone as I face an enemy
That stalks mankind
Especially those too busy
To be vigilant
And protect from its invasion
Of their peace.

They have fears.
I always discover that the men
I know and love have fears.
But I discover to my surprise
That I have fears as well:
Lack of trust
Fear of weakness
Anxiety about flooded consciousness
Concern about the unknown
Distractions and pressures
These are just a few
Of the most persistent ones.

But I discover again, as I always do,
That true love never fears
And I have company on every path
   to progress
Or to pass through pain.
I do not walk alone on this journey:
The sun rises each morning –
Sometimes teasing with passing clouds
On the heavenly playground –
Often bright in ecstasy.
The green of the growing things,
And the color of the change,
The sound of the stream at melting snowfall,
The scurry of the unseen small ones.
All these are with me daily.
Someone always hears and comforts.
My soul is at peace.

*"Hill and valley, seas and constellations, are but
stereotypes of divine ideas appealing to, and answered
by the living soul of man."*   — E. H. Chapin

> *"Deep calls unto deep*
>   *at the noise of thy waterspouts:*
> *All thy waves and thy billows*
>   *are gone over me.*
> *Yet the Lord will command*
>   *his lovingkindness in the day time,*
>   *and in the night his song shall be with me,*
>   *and my prayer unto the God of my life."*
> Psalm 42:7-8

"Then comes the father of the tempest forth,
Wrapped in black glooms. First, joyless rains obscure
Drive through the mingling skies with vapor foul,
Dash on the mountain's brow, and shake the woods
That grumbling wave below. The unsightly plain
Lies a brown deluge; as the low-bent clouds
Pour flood on flood, yet unexhausted still
Combine, and deepening into night, shut up
The day's fair face."
        from "The Seasons"
        — James Thomson

"While Spring shall pour his showers,
*   as of the wont,*
And bathe thy breathing tresses, meekest Eve!
While Summer loves to sport
Beneath thy lingering light;
While sallow Autumn fills thy lap with leaves;
Or Winter, yelling through the troublous air,
Affrights thy shrinking train,
And rudely rends thy robes;
So long, ... shall Fancy,
Friendship, Science, rose-lipped Health
Thy gentlest influence own,
And hymn thy favorite name!"

from "Ode to Evening"

— William Collins

"Yes, I remember when the changeful earth
*   ...had stamped*
The faces of the moving year, even then
I held unconscious intercourse with beauty
Old as creation, drinking in a pure
Organic pleasure from the silver wreaths
Of curling mist, or from the level plain
Of waters colored by impending clouds."

— William Wordsworth

Not Alone

"Suffering produces endurance, and endurance, character, and character, hope."
Paul's letter to the church in Rome

Recovery

Healing is such a slow, time-consuming, tiring process.
On my first walk after surgery
I noticed several long dewberry vines
   covered with tiny reddening berries.
As I continue to see them on my daily walks,
I see that very few have reached
   their sun-ripened black sweetness.
I must wait patiently for them to ripen
As I must wait patiently for my body to heal.
There is no other way.
Even in optimum circumstances,
Nature will have its own way
And do its job perfectly
And at its pre-established pace.
I cannot use any means of persuasion
   to hurry the process.
I can only use well the time it takes.

Learning

On retreat today I walked up mountain
To the prayer garden.
On the crest of the hilltop
Among the towering oaks and maples
Stood several gray-green majestic stones –
Some larger than an elephant.
Embedded in a section of one massive stone
Was the trunk of an elm tree –
Three roots straddling a lower portion.

Growth

Nearby was the gnarled root system
Of a fallen evergreen –
Beautiful in its intricate, intertwined woody core.
Twisted in varied hues of brown,
   muddy orange and sienna.

It had taken a lifetime to form that root system:
That vibrant tree sending tiny rootlets
   here and there
Seeking a hold for the storms of life
And an increased water supply from the ground
Surrounding these hardened masses.
And then years passed as the tree aged, fell,
And began the long decaying process
Until only these lovely brown root bones
Were left to demonstrate the hard work
   done by the sapling.

Time
And these majestic gray-green stones
Were not dropped from heaven.
Eons ago they were deposited
In the bowels of the earth
Under the ground that became
   this magnificent mountain.
And little-by-little, as the centuries passed
The upheavals came to stand them upright,
And the top soil washed away.
And the wind and rain rubbed them smooth
And deposited the sand at their base
And turned them from white to gray
And the green puffs of moss
And brown tatters of lichens attached
   to their thin stone skin.
Some of the stones appear to be small,
Quite easy to pick up,
But they are the noses of more massive stone
Hiding beneath mounds of earth
And waiting for future generations
To discover them and marvel at their size.

The trees grew up
Around these stones and among them,
And at last people discovered them
And created a prayer garden in their midst.

Healing
And so what is this TIME I am concerned about?
Creating and healing and change take time:
Sometimes eons, sometimes decades
   and sometimes weeks.
Now I am healing and creating and changing,
And I am not alone.

"Nature gives to every time and season
some beauties of its own;
And from morning to night,
As from the cradle to the grave,
Is but a succession of changes
So gentle and easy
That we can scarcely mark their progress."
      — Charles Dickens

"Hearing your words, and not a word among them
Tuned to my liking, on a salty day
When inland woods were pushed
  by winds that flung them
Hissing to leeward like a ton of spray,
I thought how off Matinicus the tide
Came pounding in, came running through the Gut,
While from the Rock the warning whistle cried,
And children whimpered, and the doors blew shut;
There in the autumn when the men go forth,
With slapping skirts the island women stand
In gardens stripped and scattered, peering north,
With dahlia tubers dripping from the hand:
The wind of their endurance, driving south,
Flattened your words against your speaking mouth."
— Edna St. Vincent Millay

"The man who can really, in living union of the mind
and heart, converse with God through nature, finds in
the material forms around him, a source of power and
happiness inexhaustible, and like the life of angels....
And when this grandeur of sensibility to him, and this
power of communion with him is carried, as the habit of
the soul, into the forms of nature, then the walls of our
world are as the gates of heaven."
— G. B. Cheever

Blackberry Pie

Picking blackberries today
I thought how similar the experience is
To developing a loving relationship.
The berries are so luscious and beg to be picked.
Many of them have darted
From the sheltering leaves around them
To stretch – bright and full – toward the sun.
But some of the juiciest berries
Are hidden and difficult to retrieve.

Not all berries ripen at the same time.
In fact, the bright red ones – which are the prettiest –
Are hard, sour and no good in their present state.
So picking berries for a pie requires several visits –
Several sorties into the known and reaching
Far back into the unknown to reveal a glory.

And if the ripened berries are not picked in time,
They will be enjoyed by someone else, or
They will drop to the ground,
And no one will savor their sweetness.
The best these decaying berries can do
Is to provide fertilizer for the soil
And seeds of understanding
For a future year's growth.

Just so, there are personal things
To reveal in a relationship.
Neglecting them
Will leave the experience unfulfilled.
Picking too early,
   not often enough
   or too late
Leaves it sour.

Withdrawing from a relationship
Is similar to retreating from a berry vine as well.
The berry thorns curve backward,
So jerking away leads to tearing and pain,
But gently easing away –
Sometimes coming closer for a bit –
Provides a simpler exit.
(Though the vines attempt to tear your clothes off –
Just as certain people do.)

Looking at my pricked and stained hands,
I realize that one does not leave the experience unscathed.
There are a few thorns to remove later, as well
After they have revealed their presence unexpectedly.

But the joys of a blackberry pie
Fresh from the oven
Eaten in delight
With ice cream – and friends –
Far outweighs the challenge of the gathering of the fruit!

Memory Beach

"And he called the name Rehoboth; 'for the Lord has made room for us, and we shall be fruitful in the land.'" Genesis 26:22

The Dawning
Why is it that you can hear the surf pounding on the shore –
Crashing and receding – moment by moment everlastingly,
And your ear catches the cries of the sea gulls
Swinging over your head and dipping
In their morning bath to catch breakfast,
And the orange-white glow of the early sun
Makes long shadows with your pen on the notebook,
And the sand is smooth as smooth,
And the sky is pale pink and light blue
Turning to darker blue with a white horizon.
You can feel the moisture in the air
And the wind whipping your hair,
And the chill of the spring morning –
All this you must memorize because you cannot tape it;
You cannot photograph it.
It is here in the present as it has never been before –
And will never be again – not even in five minutes.

The Vision
The subtle colors: the green algae
   on the farthest rocks of the jetty,
The pale blue of the sheen left on the sand
   as the tide leaves the beach,
The fluffy white that accompanies each incoming billow,
The dark blue and white streaks that distinguish the horizon,
The misty shrimpers far at sea,
The incredible coloring of the fishing birds,
The transparent green quality of the mounting waves
   just before they crash,
The sepia tan of the sandy beach,
The dark green of the scrubby bushes on the edge of the beach,
The gray boulders of the jetty
   and grayer wood of the worn buildings:
It is all so natural, so soft, so beautiful.

It knocks gently
On the door of your heart
And you must let it in –
Just like you must let love in –
Because it will be so wonderful
To have its presence in your life.
You must let it in:
It is too beautiful to escape unknown.

The Purpose

I come to the sea to meet my lover.
And he comes too,
Worshipping as I worship at this glad hour.
But he has his own thoughts, his own plans.
He is sharing ideas with the universe
At this threshold I call memory beach.
He is quiet: thinking, murmuring, questioning, longing.
I know not what is in his mind.
But I honor his time alone with this point
On the earth's doorway
Which he holds more sacred than life.
And it is teeming with life.
The sea gulls draw life from the ocean, their playground
And their succor: their source.
They call and cry overhead,
And they dispute territory on the shore.
There is endless beach, but still they cry and worry.
There will soon be young ones to feed.
There will soon be new life on the shore.
And the beach is teeming with sea creatures –
I right a young horseshoe crab, about the size of my thumb,
And he aims his baby waddle back to the sea
Whom he calls mother.
The jetty itself is never dry – never without life.

The tip – which thrusts its way into the life-giving ocean –
Is covered with the smooth, green life of seaweed.
And the farthest rocks are covered – simply covered –
With tiny, jet black clam shells.
They can only feed when the tide is high.
And the birds must delight in their succulence –
For several shells are empty.
But the skeleton shells are attached forever –
And black against the raging sea, they cling.

The Introduction

He is there on the jetty, thinking his thoughts,
Worshipping in his own way.
So I stay at the shore quietly singing
My morning song to the sea.
At last his service is ending,
And he turns to leave this cathedral at the shore,
So I come to the jetty to take his place.
We pass, and I speak, something, nothing,
I don't remember what I said.
But he answers! We have never met before,
But we discover that secretly,
Quietly, faithfully, we worship the sea
And honor its place in our lives.
And we each find that the other is a child of nature,
As we know ourselves to be.
We speak intimately of our cathedrals –
The mountains, the rivers, other shores.
But this one place – where I have never been before –
Is his very favorite place on earth –
The place that holds his life's treasure.
And will, he hopes, for eternity.
And I – who have spent many dawns walking on many shores –
Have discovered someone who can share my secrets.
So we – who have only just seen each other's faces
But have known the same deepest love
For as long as we can remember – we talk.
He shares his deepest secrets – his body vibrant
From his exhilarating time in his temple,

His interlude with peace and joy.
And I confide confidently my deepest thoughts –
My face radiant with the joy of being
Where I long most to be.
Here we can be what we are the most deeply.
We do not need to qualify as lovers.
We do not even need to pass the tests of true friendship.
We met each other at a place of indescribable beauty
In the temple of our God
We met. And that is enough.

The Future

I tread the sand lightly enjoying its shifting solidity
But wishing to leave it undisturbed.
The waves leave a watery sheen on the beach
Which reflects sometimes the sky,
Sometimes the shining path to the rising sun,
Sometimes the rainbow mist of the sea.
We part, pledging to find one another again at tomorrow's dawn.
And we do.

On this beach I met someone who was absorbed in his
isolation, as I was that morning. He was undergoing a personal
crisis and was haunted by the fear that no one would scatter his
ashes here – his favorite place on earth. Perhaps he was haunted
too by fear of death itself. However, when we met, we cast all
fear aside and joyed with one another in the eternal secret
sharing of *soul mates*. We soon discovered that, despite our
differences, we both were close to our Earth mother, and so we
felt ourselves to be precious children in her care. We talked
long of the rich solitude of pleasure in nature's cathedrals. As it
happened, his residence was only a few miles from my house,
although we were both far from home. But he was living in a
world that usually excluded people like me. I never saw him
again after I left the beach. But I don't need to. We met on that
joyous dawning. Our souls sang in joyful harmony.
And that is enough.

"Surely it is God who saves us.
I will trust in him and not be afraid
For the Lord is my stronghold
  and my sure defense,
And he shall be my savior.
With joy I shall draw up the water
Out of the wells of salvation,
And in that day we shall say,
Praise to the Lord
And call upon his name."
Song of Isaiah 12:2-4

"Never resting time leads summer on
To hideous winter and confounds him there,
Sap checked with frost and lusty leaves quite gone,
Beauty o'ersnowed and bareness everywhere.
Then, were not summer's distillation left, …
Beauty's effect with beauty were bereft, …
But flowers distilled, though they with winter meet,
Leese but their show; their substance
    still lives sweet."
"Then let not winter's ragged hand deface
In thee thy summer ere thou be distilled:
Make sweet some vial; treasure thou some place
With beauty's treasure ere it be self-killed."
            — William Shakespeare

"There is no trifling with nature;
It is always true, grave and severe;
It is always in the right,
And the faults and errors fall to our share.
It defies incompetency, but reveals
It's secrets to the competent,
The truthful, and the pure."
            — Goethe

"For thus says the Lord God, the Holy One of Israel:
'In returning and rest shall you be saved.
In quietness and in confidence
Shall be your strength'...
Therefore will the Lord wait
That he might be gracious unto you...
Blessed are all they that wait for him...
The people shall weep no more:
He will be gracious to you
At the voice of your cry;
When he shall hear it, he will answer...
Blessed are you that sow beside all waters."
Isaiah 30:15-20, 32:20

Mountain Lover

"When peace, like a river, attends my soul"

Friday

A beautiful weekend in a cabin in the Rockies.
I am filled with love and surrounded by beauty.
 I need no other source. What is it that I long for?
What is it that brings tears to my eyes
In this lonely meadow – alive with chirping birds
And canopied with a gentle blue sky?
I have no one to talk to, save in these scratchings.
And worse, no one takes the time to talk to me.
I hear the chatter on the evening porch
And have no desire to join it.
I think of the birds and squirrels I see here
And my own children – all locked
Into mutually satisfying relationships.
The women I meet are absorbed in their own lives.
The men I meet request instant symbols of closeness
Without laying and shoring and building
On a firm foundation of time,
    knowledge and experiences.
We all have needs,
But why are we so slow at matching those needs
And building a multitude of relationships
That are mutually advantageous to all?
We are afraid of our weaknesses.
We are afraid of our strengths.
The man to whom I am drawn with invisible cords
Seems to feel that he is not ready for a relationship—
With me or anyone else.
I must wait in peace.
The full moon is rising. I am enveloped in its soft light.

Saturday

The beauty is wondrous, but the greatest gift
The wilderness has to give, I believe, is the peace.
The only quarreling I have heard
In these mountains is the squirrel
Fussing at me from the safety of his tree.
I have invaded his space.
He chatters and scolds incessantly –
Until a hawk flies by – then suddenly
He is quiet. Peace returns to the meadow.
As I walk around the lake I notice a ground squirrel
Sunning himself on a rock near the water's edge.
I wonder if he is drying off after a brisk morning swim.
I slip off my hiking boots and
Wiggle my toes in the sand.
I gaze at the mountain peaks across the lake.
Someone tried to ski down the glacier yesterday
And broke open his head. The rescue crew
Had to carry him up to the peak
For the helicopter rescue.
He is recovering in the nearby hospital.
My trail mates and I could not figure out how
He got the skis up the mountain
    without being detected.
As the day moves toward noon, I drink my water
    (which a sprig of mint makes delightful
    in this mid-day heat)
And settle back with a nice lunch
As I watch the reflection of the mountain
Come and go in the lake at my feet.
I am so high above the lake that the cows
    look like big black ants.
Oh—those are big black ants.
One has just crawled up on my foot.
(As he sizes up my foot I wonder
If he is excited about the prospect
    of enough food to last the whole winter.)

A ground squirrel comes by
To check out the carrot bit I have discarded,
But he soon goes about his business.
I bury the peel for recycling and
    put away the carry-out trash.
I move closer to the sheltering rock
As the sun changes position overhead.
A cool breeze blowing off the lake chills me.
Winter will soon visit these mountains.
The grasshoppers are rattling away
    in the final summer sun rays.
They seem in a hurry – flying here and there.
The ants have discovered the bits of carrot
The squirrel rejected and
    are paring it down to size
    and carrying it off on their backs.
Do ants count as the wildlife that I am told not to feed?
Another squirrel pops out of the hole at my feet,
Runs to a nearby rock and
Turns to look at me inquiringly.
"Have you any food about you?" he seems to say
    [although why I think a Colorado squirrel
    would have a British accent is not clear].
He examines my toes, finds them unsuitable
And moves on.
I must put on my boots and return to civilization.
The path around the lake is filling with tourists,
And a baby has been crying for quite some time. I go.

Sunday
I rise in the morning darkness to drive back
To the airport for my early flight.
As I cross the porch of the cabin I gasp in wonder.
The full moon lights the camp with its radiance,
And the stars are bright.
Venus shines close – almost cuddling – the moon.
Jupiter and Mars are featured in the display.

Caseopia has moved to the zenith and Orion is up!
The first time I have seen him this season.
The sky is so dark that I can see his sword clearly.
I look toward the mountains.
A gentleness settles on my heart.
They are blue with mist and moonlight,
And lie quietly on my horizon
Like a lover – sleeping in peace.
This weekend in the mountains has been
A "tryst with true love" for me.
But my lover is the mountains, and I know
They will wait quietly for the joy of my return.
And when I come home,
The otter whose fondness I share
Brings me gently back to the joys of his presence.
I envelope him in my peace,
And we rejoice together.

Monday
As I return to sit beside the gurgling stream
In my secret place near my home
I remember something that I learned
   on the mountain:
I do not need to be in a certain, far away place
In order to revel in the gentle beauty of nature.
[A squirrel in a nearby tree interrupts
My quiet thoughts with a stream of chatter.
"The more things change,
   the more they stay the same."]
A cardinal clicks signals to its mate.
Sunlight touches its wing,
And it bursts into a short song.
The insects drone,
And birds call to one another in code.
It's good to be home again.

"Sympathy with nature is a part of the good man's religion."
   — F. H. Hedge

"O Lord, our Lord,
How excellent is your name in all the earth!
Who has set your glory above the heavens...
When I consider your heavens,
And the work of your fingers,
The moon and the stars, which you have ordained;
What is man that you are mindful of him?
And the son of man, that you visit him?
For you have made him
A little lower than the angels,
And have crowned him with glory and honor.
You have made him to have dominion
Over the works of your hands:
You have put all things under his feet."
        Psalm 8:1-6

The Treasure

You held a treasure in your hands, Jack,
And you set it on a shelf
And walked away from it.
I am special, Jack. Just as you are.
I don't know what you are thinking
Or how you are feeling
Or what plans are motivating your behavior
Because you haven't told me.
I don't want your lust;
I want your love.
I sense that you are not yet ready
To share your love with anyone.
Take your time. I am at peace with time.
But this week your behavior did not feel loving to me.
I have been kept in the dark.
You seem to have made decisions
In areas where I had a special interest.
When you are ready to talk to me
About your thoughts and feelings and plans – call.
And I will answer.

"Jack" is a universal name for man,
  as in "every man Jack of you."

"Hope deferred makes the heart sick:
But when the desire comes, it is a tree of life."
Proverbs 13:12

Autumn Rain

What a quiet comfort is rain.
It gentles the soul like a smooth, loving hand
Caressing the silky hair of a sobbing child.
It dampens sorrow and loss and quiets the heart
With its own sweet, soft melody.
The rain reflects my somber sense of being:
I am surrounded by mist and softness.
I walk in darkness seeking light.
So many name tags, so many name tags,
So many dances, so many songs.
How long must I smile
When I am too sad to think clearly?
How often must I spend time with others
While I continue alone?
I feel that the day and I are weeping in unison.
Never have I felt so much
That the whole weather system
Is tuned to my frequency.
The incessant, muted quality of the outdoor sounds
Of rain on the roof defies an English vocabulary –
We have no words for this quiet cleansing sound.
Someone has said "Cry and you cry alone."
But not today. Today the mountains and I
Are drenched with tears from the heavens.
We weep and we weep together.
The heavens cannot content themselves
Even with this steady weeping.
They seem to share the unabating quality
Of my sorrow. I face a change and a challenge.
And the heavens are begging forgiveness
For the summer drought.
Winter approaches;
The sunny warmth has ended.
At last, at last the earth grows greener
And melody returns to my soul.
Peace fills my mind and I will go on.

"My branches weigh me down, frost cleans the air,
My sky is black with small birds bearing south;
Say what you will, confuse me with fine care,
Put by my word as but an April truth—
Autumn is no less on me, that a rose
Hugs the brown bough and sighs before it goes."
— Edna St. Vincent Millay

"Time does not bring relief; you have lied
Who told me time would ease me of my pain!
I miss him in the weeping of the rain;
I want him at the shrinking of the tide;
The old snows melt from every mountain-side,
And last year's leaves are smoke in every lane;
But last year's bitter loving must remain
Heaped on my heart, and my old thoughts abide.
There are a hundred places where I fear
To go—so with his memory they brim.
And entering with relief some quiet place
Where never fell his foot or shone his face
I say, "there is no memory of him here!"
And so stand stricken, so remembering him."
        — Edna St. Vincent Millay

"Thou, O God, sent a plentiful rain,
whereby you confirmed your inheritance,
when it was weary."
Psalm 68:9

"'Stand in awe and sin not:
Commune with your own heart
Upon your bed,   and be still.'
I will both lay me down in peace,
and sleep: For you, Lord, only
make me to dwell in
safety."
Psalm 4

My Secret Place

When I am lonely
I come to this stream to wrap myself
In the refreshing arms of Nature.
She wraps her boughs around me and draws me
Close to the beating heart of the earth.
I feel, rather than see, the rhythm of all things living,
And the deeper, somber bass notes of those things
Only the geologists identify as moving.
The dappled sunlight is caught by the stream
And becomes a mirror here in the shallows,
And a cascade of shattered diamonds as it moves
Over the rounded stones that block its path.
The birds call to each other in the distance
And the cicadas perform
Their summer concert from the trees.
An early hickory nut crashes
Through the leaves to the forest floor.
A rabbit scurries
    through the last of autumn's leavings.
And I know that I am not alone.

"Set me as a seal upon thine heart,
As a seal upon thine arm:
For love is strong as death;
Jealousy is cruel as the grave...
Many waters cannot quench love,
Neither can the floods drown it:
If a man could give
All the substance of his house for love,
It would utterly be condemned...
Make haste, my beloved
And be thou like to a roe
Or to a young hart upon the mountains of spices."
Song of Solomon 8:6-7,14

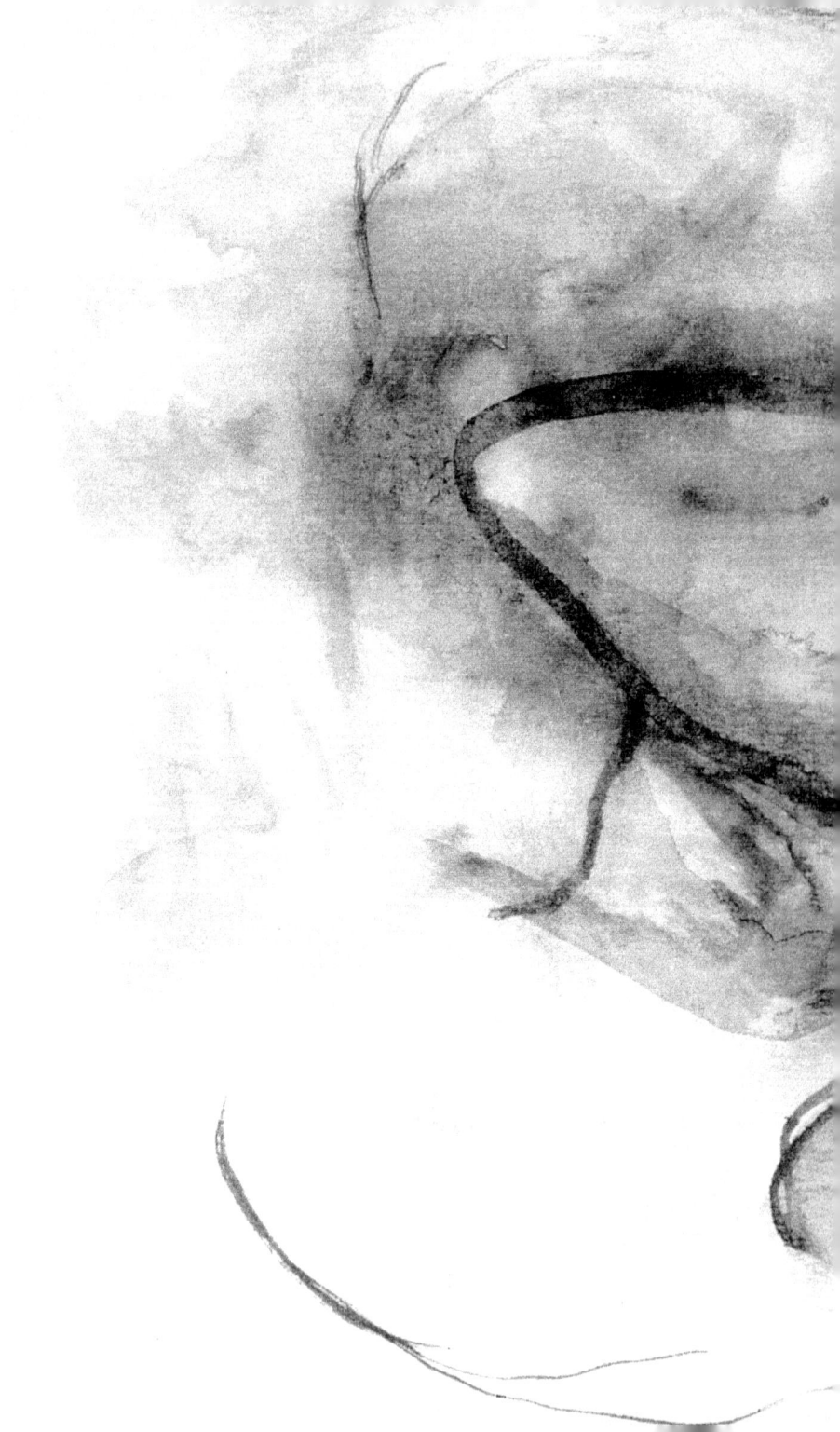

Starlight & Moonbeams

Princess

Waiting for someone special
Who sees that I am someone special
Has created a dark, warm vacuum in my heart.
My sadness is like sorrow:
A mourning for something I never had.
Thinking about emptiness brings the image
    to my mind which I had created
    during a difficult time of decision.
I am walking into a private library,
Darkened with the falling shadows of evening.
The loving father that I created for such times
    of sharing thought and wisdom
Sits in a comfortable chair beneath the only
    light in the room, reading.
He looks up as he hears my footfall on the threshold,
And a smile breaks forth on his face
    that seems to light the whole room.
He always looks up, whatever he is doing,
And he is always glad to see me,
To hear my thoughts and concerns
And share a spray of blossoms
From his vast arbor of wisdom.
He lays the book aside and takes me in his arms
    for a moment.
The warmth of his embrace
    Spreads throughout my body
And I am no longer chilled.
Then he places his large, strong hands
On my soft shoulders.
He listens long to my thoughts and desires
And pauses before answering
Like someone carefully making a selection
    for this particular need—
Just the right hue, just the right fragrance
Just the right freshness, just the right size and shape:
He searches for a response like an artist selecting materials.

As I gaze peacefully into his steady eyes,
I can guess the stringing logic
    working in his sympathetic mind.
"Had you ever thought," he says,
"How long a princess waits
    for the coming of her true love?"
"The fairy tales begin their story
    shortly before the arrival of the prince,
But she spends many, many quiet years
Learning to think, and study and understand
So that she can make wise judgments
    when she becomes a ruler.
She spends countless hours rounding and delighting
Her spirit with archery and music and sewing and art.
She walks in the meadow and the woodland
And rides horseback over the meads
So that she can know first hand the tenor of her land."
He goes on as long as I need to hear his voice,
Telling me of constructing logic and building wisdom
And growing stronger and more patient.
And these qualities, he tells me,
    are those I am developing now.
The quiet time, when there are few inter-personal demands,
Is the time for developing self-awareness and understanding.
And, growing to understand that my time
    and interests are valuable,
And most of all that I am loved,
I am content.

*"Nature imitates herself. A grain thrown into good
ground brings forth fruit; a principle thrown into a good
mind brings forth fruit. Everything is created and
conducted by the same Master—the root, the branch, the
fruits—the principles, the consequences."*
        — Pascal

Stargazer

The Preparation

It is a name. It is a short name.
But it is a name overflowing with meaning.
I am to meet him there.
We do not know each other.
I am not sure I will recognize him,
But already I am aware
Of his profound presence in my life.
It is a vibrant autumn afternoon,
And he is there – smiling.

The Meeting

I have had this experience only twice before in my life.
Both times were special.
Both times brought heart aching sweetness
Into my somber life.
Both times I was caught doing what I like best.
Both times it was an enchanting experience.
Each of those two previous times
I met someone as I wandered in nature's chapel
Where I love to worship.
And here I am today
Coming to accompany a perfect stranger
On a trip to see the stars.
Today I meet him
Before I catch a glimpse of the place of worship.
He is there to greet me.
He smiles again.
He has a warm, engaging smile.
His eyes flash
Even though the sun has gone behind a cloud.
I am calm. I am at peace.
I am with him.

The Adventure

The warm, sunny drive together
Endlessly chatting like old friends
The longed-for tour of the ancient home
Calls up memories – but not from our own experience.
The breath-taking hike up the mountain
The mysterious vista from the peak
Where all is laid out neatly before us,
The race down the hill
Through an autumn-colored landscape,
And suddenly, friends!
More fellowship for the picnic.
More smiles. More laughter.
More pleasure in simply being myself
And discovering the joy
Of being with someone who is reveling
In the pleasure of simply being himself with me!

The Wonder

And then the house lights dim
And the drama begins.
We speak in whispers
Of the majesty of God's mighty realm.
We are shown some of the mysteries –
By those who know them well.
We see Jupiter with its attending moons
All lined up for the heavenly dance.
And it disappears before we get a second glance.
But then we see the binary star
Which handles the Big Dipper.
I show him Cassiopeia at the zenith.
We do not touch – that first day –
But we think about it all the time.
Once, I reach out for his hand
To steady myself on the astronomer's stool.
And gasp at the beauty of the stars of blue and gold –
While I am thinking all the time
Of the security of his gentle hand.

The Happy Ending

We drive through the night
Continuing to discover areas of our lives
That bring each other joy.
And we stop at the meeting place
And continue to talk
Until Time reminds us that
We must be about our Father's business.
And we part – longing to see one another again.
And, Oh, Joy! Soon we dance!

"Not from the stars do I my judgment pluck,
And yet methinks I have astronomy;
But not to tell of good or evil luck,
Of plagues, of dearths, or seasons' quality;
Nor can I fortune to brief minutes tell,
Pointing to each his thunder, rain, and wind,
Or say with princes if it shall go well
By oft predict that I in heaven find;
But from thine eyes my knowledge I derive,
And, constant stars, in them I read such are
As truth and beauty shall together thrive
If from thyself to store thou woudst convert:
Or else of thee this I prognosticate,
Thy end is Truth's and Beauty's doom and date."
　　　　　— William Shakespeare

"What profusion is there in His work!
When trees blossom, there is not a single breastpin,
But a whole bosom-full of gems;
And of leaves, they have so many suits
That they can throw them away to the winds
All summer long.
What unnumbered cathedrals has He reared
    in the forest shades,
Vast and grand, full of curious carvings,
And haunted evermore by tremulous music;
And in the heavens above,
    how do stars seem to have flown
Out of His hand faster than sparks out of a mighty forge!
            — H. W. Beecher

"How beautiful are thy feet with shoes,
O prince's daughter!
The joints of thy thighs are like jewels,
The work of the hands of a cunning workman.
Thy navel is like a round goblet,
Which wants no liquor:
Thy belly is like a heap of wheat
Set about with lilies.
Thy two breasts are like
Two young roes that are twins.
Thy neck is as a tower of ivory;
Thine eyes are like the fishpools in Heshbon...
Thine head upon thee is like Carmel,
And the hair of thine head like purple,
The king is held in the galleries.
How fair and how pleasant are thou,
O Love, for delights!
This thy stature is like to a palm tree,
And thy breasts like clusters of grapes.
I said, I will go up to the palm tree.
I will take hold of the boughs thereof;
Now also thy breasts shall be as clusters of the vine,
And the smell of thy nose like apples;
And the roof of thy mouth
Is like the best wine for my beloved,
That goes down sweetly causing the lips
Of those that are asleep to speak.
I am my beloved's, and his desire is toward me."

Song of Solomon 7:1-10

Brother of the Earth

When we walk together in the open wood,
Our feet sifting through the crisp leaves,
Bright mushrooms, and unexpected blossoms,
We create a space as we walk and discuss many things.
Our talk goes on for hours – literal, spiritual, emotional,
Sexual, physical, intellectual, social.
We speak at times and we listen at times,
But always we attend to that other voice:
The voice of the small creatures flying or singing near us.
We stop our conversation and listen to theirs.
We watch their smallest movement for a time,
My body pressed against your arm
As I steady the binoculars.
You tell me the names of the ones I have not met,
And I interpret their language to you.
We take a space, then walk and talk again.
We enjoy the magnificent vision of the sun
Setting in muted glory behind the dark trees
That shelter the gray lake.
We turn and begin our homeward journey.
And on that journey
You provide from your goodness for me,
And I provide from my goodness for you.
You find the wrongs and right them:
You mend this and fix that and suggest the other.
Where there is concern, you are there
To lead the way to peace.
I prepare a repast that fills you and warms you
And delights you in its own way.
I cradle your foot in my hands, and—
listening to its soft voice –
I coax it back to health.
We work together, we two,
and form a partnership in provision.

Fear sometimes grows like a weed vine in the meadow:
Threatening, circling, choking the young plants
That seek the sunlight of love.
There are times apart, and during those times
Anxiety smothers growth
Like ice crystals during a late winter storm:
Present, past and future abandonment; dishonesty;
Lack of clarity; lack of control; losses;
Enmeshment; powerlessness; helplessness; hopelessness;
Come crowding each other in their effort to
Overcome the innocent heart.
Hope, power, love, purpose, strength, wisdom,
Decision, perception, choice
Flood the soul and battle the fears
That have attempted residence in our being.
And at last peace returns to the meadow.

Brother of the Earth,
The rugged beauty of your massive gentleness
Draws me to you.
Fold me softly into the warm cave
Closest to your vibrant heart.
As I enter I find that you have prepared
This place for my coming
With scented candles to light the corners
And share their fragrance with our souls.
The fire which draws me in
Creates a circle of safety with its light.
It warms the cave and amazes us
With its ever-changing presence,
Glowing and murmuring as a living thing.
The fire gives off its own fragrance –
Smells from the fruits of the woodland of its infancy
And the fallen leaves from the winter of our lives.
For softness at my feet
Your own living body to cushion my head at rest.
As I explore the depths I find living moss.
You cradle my head with the strength of your arm
And smooth my silken hair as you tell me stories.

You tell me stories about you, and me, and us, and joy,
And peace, and fullness, and thoughts and passion.
Your hand plays with my clothing and before long
Your firm hand is smoothing
   the knotted muscles of my back.
They relax in peace at your touch.
Your soul rejoices at seeing
   my bare back in the firelight.
Your eyes shine as your face succumbs
To the onslaught of my tender kisses.
You engage my mind with your soliloquy
As you engage my body with your caress.
Place your soul in your hand
   and rub it like oil on my body.
I rejoice at your touch and my supple body
Absorbs your attention
   and remains alert to your pleasure.
I take your place of honor, and
You attend warmly to my caress,
Your body vibrant with hope.
You voice the images
That are thrusting themselves into your mind.
Shimmering on the verge of consciousness,
The image ignites your thinking
And sets fire to your composure,
Thrusting itself in and in and further in.
The poetic parts of your body tingle with anticipation
At having their time of warmth and attention.
Your body becomes like a clamoring classroom –
Each part vying for the lasting pleasure of my tenderness.
You seek instruction
   in what you already know but long for;
You ask permission to practice endlessly, endlessly
Until we are abated. Outside, the sun sets.
Inside, we spend hours enveloped
   in one another's warmth. Then, as Orion appears
  and the blue moon rises to guide us,
We begin a time apart.
Hoping to be together soon again.

November Notes

❧   **Thank you for**

the woodland morning glories
the gentle murmur of waking birds
the sun's radiance sweeping away the clouds
   in the morning sky
the tree that stands alone in the distant mist
the call of the migrating geese
the vast grassy field with dew on every blade
the vibrant red field flowers
   against the golden harvest grain
the last summer song of the evening cricket

❧   **Thank you for**

the vast, powerful, gray-green ocean
the ever-pounding surf
the raucous call of sea birds
the strong, salty wind
the mounds of shifting sand
the radiant clouds
the golden sun rising
   in the eternal depth of sky

❧   **Thank you for**

shocking reality
the comfort of structure
invigorating freedom
the awareness of pain
the confrontation of anger
the path-altering terror of fear
challenging ideas
soul-searching questions
solid, vibrant answers
patience
time

❦   Thank you for
the streamside evenings
the quiet green of moss-covered stumps
the tiny purple blossoms
   hidden under emerald leaves
the promising beauty
   of shiny chocolate colored acorns
   crashing through the branches above
the spotted cranberry mushrooms
   flinging up white petticoats
   in their dance on the forest floor
the clarity, purity and power
   of the ever-gurgling brook
the occasional note of a bird
   or crack of a tree limb
the continuous hum
   of the late summer insects
the cold, massive, rugged beauty
   of gray-green boulders
the curious spider walk
   of a granddaddy-long-legs
the tiny soft, brown rustle
   of a chipmunk in the fallen leaves
the soft round darkness of an animal's den
the warm, rough embrace with a water elm
the colorful glory of changing leaves
the last filtered shaft of daylight through the trees

Good night

Sorrows by Streamside

Streamside Memories

The woodland stream provides a steady joy,
Surrounds my soul with comfort,
And nurtures my life with peace.
What a miracle to find something steady and beautiful –
Ever changing and always the same.
The rhythm and melody of the rushing water
Soothes the body,
Relaxes the muscles and quiets the mind.
Noisy, it is a place of quiet
To contemplate the joys of last night:
Thoughts which were closeted during the day
But now, as evening approaches,
Are allowed to wander freely in the hallways of my mind.
The peace, the smooth quality of the silky skin,
The sudden joy of being.
To see your pleasure, to hear your sigh,
To accept your kisses and force more on you.
To be close
And to be at peace where there is no rancor:
Softness, smooth and gentle, invites you closer.
Firmness, oiled and vibrant invades and conquers.
And here today on the bank
I see old rocks; smooth rocks,
Bridled by small greenness,
Which buries the banks.
The din of water melody fills my ears.

"'Twas autumn, and a clear and placid day,
With warmth, as much as needed, from a sun
Two hours declined toward the west; a day
With silver clouds, and sunshine on the grass,
And in the sheltered and the sheltering grove
A perfect stillness."
— William Wordsworth

Mountain Thoughts

"Be still and know that I am God."
Psalm 46:10

"Absorb the peace. Inhale the quiet. Do not seek.
Do not give. Rest in my provision for you."
This is the message for me at this season.
I am sitting "up mountain" on a rock
Above the camp in the early dawn.
The mountains are just cresting pink on their somber gray image.
My mind is full of observances, but I am reminded
To let my mind rest. My heart is filled with praise:
"Oh, Lord, My God, when I in awesome wonder
consider all the worlds thy hands have made..."
But I need rest,
And I hear the inner command not to speak or sing.

I hear the hunting birds calling
To one another in this early stillness.
The tiny song birds in the nearby pine
Twitter and chatter to one another.
The pink brightness of the early dawn moves slowly
Down the mountainside,
And now it is lighting the quiet town nestled at its feet.
There is a cry for help from the nearby ridges. Stillness.
Then a high-pitched horse's whinny.
Suddenly voices from all four ridges answer the call.
Wolves howl and seem to be rushing
To the site of the first voice –
Though no movement can be detected
Through the thick trees.
One learns a lot about wolves
When one visits their high mountain home.

At last the brightness at the topmost ridge
Lights my meadow with sunlight
And warms my shoulders with its glory.
My mind absorbs and responds to its surroundings,

But I understand that I am not yet ready to analyze or write.
At this time I am cradled in God's goodness
And nurtured by mother Earth. I am at peace.

A ground squirrel – looking like a chipmunk –
Awakens in this sunlight and clucks from its hole.
A tiny, quick bird alights on the branch near my head
To check me out.
He soon returns to his fellows with his message.
What is his message, I wonder?
They spiral up the dying tree nearby, twittering all the way.

Gray birds are scavenging among the seeded grasses.
The breeze stirs the grass heads ever so gently.
I munch quietly on Tropical Trail Mix
And set the bag on the ground beside me
As I sink back into reverie.
A moment later I notice movement at my elbow.
The ground squirrel is deep into my trail mix.
He looks up at me as if to say, "I know that the signs say
Do Not Feed the Wild Animals,
But do I look like a wild animal to you?
I'm less than three inches away from you,
And how could I harm a giant like you?"
He persuades me to his logic, and I swear him to secrecy.
He dives back into the seed and dried fruit mixture,
Backing off only when I reach in for my share.
He picks up a piece of guava, tastes it, spits it out
And throws the large, orange piece away.
Soon his pouches are so full that he looks like someone
With a bad toothache.
I explain to him that his body was not built
To hold any more food, and I put the bag away.
He climbs up on my shoulder as a better vantage point
For locating additional food.
Disappointed, he searches my knapsack. I zip it closed,
And he scampers away.
I hear him telling a friend of his good fortune.

I look around this crest and see tiny desert flowers
Pocked everywhere: blue brushes, gray sage, white stars,
lavender bonnets, yellow daisies, purple asters.
The grasses are thin and half brown
After baking in the summer sun for many days.
Gray and green ground covers hug the earth
Between the tufts – laying low to avoid the extremes
Of winter cold and summer heat at this altitude.
The leaves on the bushes are shiny and small
For the same reason.
All is poised and ready in this stillness
Before the harsh winter begins to take its toll.

Where is the water? There are waterfalls
And cascading streams less than a mile away
"As the crow flies," and a native says
That it rained every day during July.
The counselor at the camp says to hike early
Because afternoon showers are common here.
But still the landscape appears parched.
The gathered waters are deeply underground.
This is a fragile environment.

A hawk flies overhead, beating the air with his wings.
A woodpecker has found the dying tree.
A squirrel in another tree flashes his tail
Like a matador's cape.
What is he signaling, I wonder?
I realize that I look at the natural world
To discover truths in my own life, and I discover
How I have moved my focus from those truths.

I think about how fragile man is:
"What is man that Thou are mindful of him?"
We surround ourselves with artificial beauty and favors –
Just as this upland meadow decorates itself with flowers –
But we, like it, are very fragile.
A little carelessness can cause great loss.

The guide says that it takes 40 years up here
To recover from a fire.
We may have to spend years repairing a loss.
It may never be fully repaired.
And if we are diligent and hardworking,
An "act of God" may still destroy or remove our treasures.
And we discover (to our surprise) that we are fragile –
Just like this mountain environment.

I note, too, that God gave us needs for sustenance
Which must come from outside sources –
Just as this meadow needs warmth, water,
And reprieve from both of them –
And it has no control over this provision.

We sometimes *feel* powerless, but we discover,
As we continue to learn, adjust and grow, that it is not so.
After a while we say to ourselves,
"If I could survive *that*, I can survive anything,"
And we gain confidence.
I look at the twisted, living trees
And hear them telling the young saplings,
"If I could survive the winter of '88,
This winter will not kill me.
I cracked the rock and sunk my roots deep
For just such a time as this."

We learn that our temporal experiences
Are not attached to our Essential Self.
They come and go in our existence.
We discover that
Those who truly love us are not concerned
With the externals we don for various occasions.
We are shocked to learn that some of the treasures
We have lost were not treasures at all.
And so, little by little, *"line by line, line by line"*
We discover that we can be content –
Even at peace and happy – even after a terrible loss,
Even knowing that our future is riddled with other losses.

We know that *"God's in his heaven, all's right with the world."*
Looking again at this mountain meadow filled with warmth
And light and many living creatures,
I see that it, too, is fragile, but resilient.
I begin to understand that God designed his creation
To keep struggling regardless of difficulties
And then to rejoice, bloom, sing and thrive
Whenever we creatures receive the nurture we need.

This meadow has survived another of the endless summers
That have visited these young mountains.
It will survive yet another harsh winter
And still bloom to tell the story.
It will bloom and thrive. And so will I.
The peace of the mountain meadow returns to my heart.

"Up mountain" is a Scottish term used to mean a pilgrimage,
not only up the mountain during a time of seeking, but nearer to God,
the source of all wisdom.

> *"When the poor and needy seek water,*
> *And there is none, and their tongue fails for thirst,*
> *I the Lord will hear them,*
> *I the God of Israel will not forsake them.*
> *I will open rivers in high places,*
> *And fountains in the midst of the valleys.*
> *I will make the wilderness a pool of water.*
> *I will plant in the wilderness the cedar,*
> *The acacia tree and the myrtle and the oil tree;*
> *I will set in the desert the fir tree,*
> *And the pine, and the box tree together."*
> Isaiah 41:17-19

"Surely there is something in the unruffled calm of nature
that overawes our little anxieties and doubts: the sight of the
deep-blue sky, and the clustering stars above, seem to impart
a quiet to the mind."
— Jonathan Edwards

"Nature has perfections, in order to show
That she is the image of God;
And defects, to show that she is only an image."
    — Pascal

"I follow nature as the surest guide,
And resign myself, with implicit obedience,
To her sacred ordinances."
    — Cicero

"Nature has nothing made so base,
But can read some instruction
To the wisest man."
— C. Aleyn

"Nature is too thin a screen;
The glory of the One breaks in everywhere."
— Emerson

Winter Reverie

The Woodlands
The winter quiet of the woods:
The stream bed choked by fallen leaves –
Already colored earth-somber
For their reintegration into the womb that bore them.
The fitful breeze brushing the tips of the trees,
The water laughing gaily at it runs rampant over the rocks
And falling silent when it is trapped in the eddies.
The animals silently preparing for winter famine.
A leaf spiraling earthward in its innocent beauty.
The barren woods pierced by a shaft of mellow gold
From the sun – already barred from the zenith –
So that the scene looks more like an afternoon tavern
Than a cloudless morning.
Life's Journey
I can go anywhere.
I can do anything.
Do I want to return to the land of my youth
Where the sun brings dazzling warmth
Through all the seasons?
Shall I bide at the foot of the mountains
That whisper softly in my dreams?
Shall I flee the city for a simpler life?
Patient Waiting
Thought: a farmer busies himself with daily tasks
While he awaits the gentle growth
Of the seeds he planted in hope.
He watches as they nose their way out of the soil,
Spread, bud, and ripen
Into a new crop to harvest.
So also must I wait for more information,
For wisdom, for leadership,
And I must also attend to the life
That is set before me today.
I go to drink the day's cup.

Weeding in the Morning

Relationships with people are a lot like gardening.
Sometimes the soil must be prepared
And extensive work done before anything will grow.
Certain plants will not grow in certain climates.
Some plants take two or more years of preparation
Before producing.
Openness, coolness and availability are essential.
Nurture, like water, fertilizer and care, encourages.
Weeding is always necessary in a relationship.
Weeds are more easily removed
When they are not deeply embedded,
Clinging to soil or intertwined
Among healthy plants with similar characteristics.

"How thick about us root, how rankly grow
Those subtle weeds no man has need to tend,
That flourish through neglect, and soon must send
Perfume too sweet upon us and overthrow
Our steady senses; how such matters go
We are aware, and how such matters end."
— Edna St. Vincent Millay

"There is so much in the world for us all if we only have
the eyes to see it, and
the heart to love it, and
the hand to gather it to ourselves."
– Lucy Maud Montgomery

Paths

"You will show me the path that leads to life."

I am on a mountain holiday
Alternating hiking with photography.
I stop to note the surprising wonders
I find along my path:
A hollow log, filled with shelf fungi –
As if someone has set up housekeeping –
One tiny, arrow-straight, brown mushroom
On a huge decaying log,
A tiny green cup mushroom
Forming an intricate design with varied mosses,
A half-dozen red and yellow leaves
Turned into Valentines,
A weathered stone snuggly covered
In soft ferns and mosses.

This is the last day of my mountain retreat.
The first few days were filled with friends and frolic,
The next two days revolved around
A dear friend whom I probed
For answers to the questions
That have haunted me since I have known him.
And now I am alone "up mountain"
Wandering in God's bounty,
Drinking deeply of the beauty that surrounds me.
Which path shall I take?

> *"Love one another...*
> *Aspire to live quietly,*
> *To mind your own affairs,*
> *And to work with your hands*
> *As we have charged you,*
> *That you may walk honestly*
> *Toward them that are without,*
> *And you may have lack of nothing."*
> I Thessalonians 4:9,11-12

"To Love
is to allow another person
to make a real difference
in one's life,
and because of the difference
the other person makes,
to act toward that person
so as to assist him or her
to develop more fully as a person."
from Loving Yourself as Your Neighbor
by Mark Taylor and Carmen Berry

"Thou art fairer than the children of men:
Grace is poured into thy lips:
Therefore God has blessed thee for ever.
Gird thy sword...
In your majesty ride forth victoriously
For the cause of truth
And defend the right...
All thy garments smell of myrrh,
And aloes and cassia,
Out of the ivory palaces
Whereby they have made thee glad...
Hearken, O daughter, and consider,
And incline thine ear;
Forget thine own people,
And thy father's house;
So shall the King
Greatly desire thy beauty..."
Psalm 45, selected verses

Fresh Vision

Written on a Christmas Morning

There are times when the big, exciting distractions of fun,
Family and friends are not available.
It is in those times that I notice the simple, joyous pleasures
That are always available
And continue to make life a marvelous experience.
There are always advantages to not having all that one wants.
When distractions are cleared away, one discovers
That there is still substantial beauty
And value readily available in one's life.
It is when the beautiful, vibrant leaves fall from the limbs
That we see the intricate silhouette of the majestic tree
Finely etched against the sky.
When no one makes their way to my house
Or calls on a bright, cloudless day –
The birds still greet me from the birdfeeder, glad
For a friend who cares for them in the 20 degree weather.
When no one sends a message of their continuing love,
The sun still brightens my life every morning –
No matter how I am feeling within.
And in the evening, another gift without a visible giver:
The night quietly closes out all daily problems,
And sleep comes to "knit the raveled sleeve of care."
I find that I am indeed resilient
Regardless of the problems faced.
Season after season cool breezes relieve the heat
And a bright sun warms up an icy environment.
When not called on for other duties,
I enter a period of timelessness and enjoy its freedoms.
Whatever is happening in my life,
The gift of music is always available –
From the radio, at a concert, in the choir –
These are ready joys for everyone.
It is said, "music is the only paradise
From which man cannot be driven."
Intricate melody and rhythm play in my head
When my body isn't moving –

And sometimes encourages me to cast aside my lethargy
And dance along.
My body longs for food, and this is a gift too,
For I can explore new avenues of taste
Or visit familiar haunts of favorite meals.
I learn to care tenderly and thoughtfully for myself:
To listen when my body speaks. My body stays in rhythm –
The greater and lesser rhythms of the universe
Play themselves out in the finite bodies of the earthbound.
We are moving with the music of the spheres
Whether we realize it or not.
(And the universe is not concerned
About whether or not we are aware of it.)
And I can always walk in the wilderness of created things –
Even if I must hobble like a blind peddler with a stick
On icy paths as I did today in the white wonder
That was my garden.
The qualities of nature are delightful and endless –
A bird on the wing, ice glinting in the winter sun,
A few green leaves clustered on a young bush,
A squirrel caught dashing to check on his winter hoard
While pretending to be playing a carefree game.
Warm, soft pets listen peacefully to our talk –
Both those that purr or bark
And those inanimate ones that nestle snuggly without a sound
In an overstuffed chair by the fireplace.
Quiet friends are waiting for visits in many places.
Retirement homes and hospitals are full of beautiful people
Who would like a visit with someone enjoyable.
Children's hugs and delighted faces are always available –
The day-care centers are longing for an adult to come in
And read to the young children,
And the church nursery can always use help in cradling,
Feeding and nurturing their precious ones.
Every day children integrate delighted surprise
In the common things in their lives. Each day is new.
They have little experience of gain, so each simple addition
To their lives is received with interest and joy.

They are closely aware of reality –
Especially the simplest, most obvious parts –
And have no shame about discussing clear facts.
"Clarity of perception and accuracy of response"
Is typical for children.
Love is "clarity of perception and accuracy of response."
Children represent love on this earth.
Children do not worry about yesterday or tomorrow;
They simply love today
And the presence of each one of us in it.
We can all become like children as well.
And it is good.

> *"Truly I say to you,*
> *Unless you turn and become as a little child,*
> *You shall not enter into the kingdom of heaven.*
> *Whoever therefore shall humble himself*
>   *as a little child,*
> *The same is greatest in the kingdom of heaven."*
> Matthew 18:3-4

Chocolate Dessert and Strawberry Kisses

Dancing, dancing, dancing, dancing!
The music whirls around me in a frenzy of gaiety.
I am with the man who has taught me to appreciate dancing.
For the first time I do not feel alone on the swirling dance floor.
He smiles and he dances and holds me in joy.
We dance away together the last afternoon hours
of the last century of our lives—
The first year of the new millennium is only a few hours away.
There is a rush and excitement
Other dancers join us in rejoicing in these final active hours.

But we do not stay in the moving musical joy.
The skies are darkening, and we are off to other adventures.
We find coldness and darkness and friendship and warmth.
We cradle the chili, and comfort our hands.
We cuddle in the back of a drafty tent
Listening to young folks make music from metal cans.
We wander again in icy darkness
And discover a warm darkness
With music for dancing,
And up we rise and dancing we do.

Once again a cold windy darkness leads us to more joy.
Bluegrass rhythms raise our spirits
And we settle in warmth for joy upon joy.
At last, at last, frozen to the core
We take ourselves away—
Forsaking the celebration fireworks on the cold, windy deck.
We refresh ourselves with chocolate before a roaring fire.
When midnight strikes (a little late),
We share kisses all around
And head sleepily to our rest.
Tiny dots of starlight
Shine outside my window.
Orion sheds his blessing on my bed,
And I sleep in peace.

Another day comes with excitement in the air.
We settle quietly around the fire
And share fellowship with friends.
And when the friends leave to follow
The leadings of their own lives,
We two are left sharing chocolate desserts
   and strawberry kisses.
We dance by the fire—just the two of us—slowly.
Time dictates a quiet closing to this blessing
And we retire to rest.
My window looks out on nothing but white.
The safe haven of this house is surrounded by snow.
All night long the snow keeps falling ~ softly, silently.
My eyes close gently, and I am asleep.

"Nature is beautiful, always beautiful!
Every little flake of snow is a perfect crystal,
And they fall together as gracefully
As if fairies of the air caught water drops
And made them into artificial flowers
To garland the wings of the wind."
        — Mrs. L. M. Child

Fickle Weather

Although winter was more than a memory,
A spring breeze seemed to brush my cheek,
And the sun warmed my soul
When you came into my life
And asked to stay.

The winter had been long and cold.
My laughter had often died on my lips
During that season of loss.
I had lost everything – my home, my community,
My security and those I loved.
The damp air and unforgiving wind
Had often tried to penetrate my heart
And bring into my self its icy comfort.

You met me on an icy evening
And shared your specialty with all –
But you held your eyes on me,
And your warm attention
Brought spring into my being.
Heart echoed heart in our meeting
And our joy was full.

You called often, and we talked long.
We shared our triumphs and our tragedies.
We agreed to meet soon again.
The chives in my garden felt the warm promise.
And began their hopeful journey to the sun.
Tiny flowers began peeking from their hiding.
And signs of spring filled the air.

You filled my home with beautiful flowers.
Their precious beauty brought
The spring of my life indoors to greet me.
You showered me with your rapt attention
And sheltered me with your kiss.

We holidayed together and took joy in future promises.
You didn't dance, but I did, holding you.
Our hearts danced together.
I have not been happier for many a season.

But the sleeper must wake from dreams,
And reality is sometimes a cold comfort.
Distances are long,
And journeys difficult.
Obligations creep up and bind the spirit –
Dizzy with freedom.

Another icy night came,
And the chives lost their lives in the dark.
The tiny flowers in the lawn disappeared,
And the beauties in the vase
Bowed their heads at last.
The joy could not be sustained.
Second thoughts and a freezing wind
Had reclaimed the landscape.
And now is my heart enshrouded in cold memories.
Until the spring comes once again to my soul.

"My times are in your hand."
Psalm 31:15

*"Clearly my ruined garden as it stood
Before the frost came on it I recall—
Stiff marigolds, and what a trunk of wood
The zinnia had, that was the first to fall;
These pale and oozy stalks, these hanging leaves
Nerveless and darkened, dripping in the sun,
Cannot gainsay me, though the spirit grieves
And wrings its hands at what the frost has done."*
— Edna St. Vincent Millay

*"Yours is a face of which I can forget
The colour and the features, every one,
The words not ever, and the smiles not yet;
But in your day this moment is the sun
Upon a hill, after the sun has set."*
      — Edna St. Vincent Millay

"*That time of year thou mayst in me behold*
when yellow leaves, or none, or few, do hang
Upon those boughs which shake against the cold,
Bare, ruined choirs where late the sweet birds sang."
— William Shakespeare

Jack

The morning you told me
That you didn't want to see me, Jack,
That day I went to the store
And saw pictures of couples on magazines –
Couples who were doing things
That we have never done –
Might never do
Since you have withdrawn from me.
And the man at the video store
Had his name on his lapel,
And it was your name, Jack.
And when I looked for a friend's address –
The only name I could see on the page
Was your name, Jack.
And I thought about you
And gave you space
And gave you time
And prayed for you,
And you called
And we talked
And you said…
What did you say?
Ah, Jack,
Hearing your voice again brought such joy,
I cannot remember what you said.

"By night on my bed
I sought him whom my soul loves,
I sought him, but found him not…
I will seek him whom my soul loves:
I sought him, but I found him not…
I found him whom my soul loves:
I held him, and would not let him go.
Who is this that comes out of the wilderness
Like pillars of smoke, perfumed with myrrh
And frankincense, with all powders of the merchant?"
Song of Solomon 3:1-6

Blossoms in Springtime

Poem of Promise

He came in the autumn
And stayed through the winter
And brought the warmth of summer
To my body and my soul.
He is John, God's gracious gift to me.

My love is like a meadow
Filled with bright flowers of many kinds and colors
Tossing their festive heads carelessly
In a warm and gentle breeze.
His lips are like the softest petals of a country rose.
And the fragrance of his body
Is like a cedar bathing in the summer sun.

To kiss him is to enter the soft depths of a sleeping flower.
Surrounded by gently pulsing beauty,
Soft warmth, and the sweetest fragrance of memory.
His kisses are like a garland of summer flowers.
My tongue rejoices at the nectar I find there.
Delighted giggles bubble up and spill all about us.
Caress and caring
Pleasure and softness
Spirit and light

I brush his smooth cheek with my lips,
And he turns to ask for more.
His smile is radiating from his face
Like sunbeams through a misty cloud.
His eyes shine with mischief and good times.
I exclaim and he reminds me that
"Goodness had nothing to do with it!"
The softest petals, the softest petals.
I think of kissing him and remember
Licking the nectar from honeysuckle.
To be held in his arms is security and promise.
His tender ears whet my appetite.

A cross of gold he fetched for me
Away on foreign shores.
I wear it always around my neck
To remind me of him and our Love.
The Lord of Love who brought beauty and softness
And warmth and love into our lives.
God brought me into your life to demonstrate love to you.
How am I doing?

"My beloved is white and ruddy,
 The chiefest among ten thousand.
His head is as the most fine gold,
His locks are bushy and black as a raven.
His eyes are as the eyes of doves by the rivers of waters,
 Washed with milk, and fitly set.
His cheeks are as a bed of spices, as sweet flowers:
His lips like lilies, dropping sweet smelling myrrh.
His hands are as gold rings set with the beryl.
His belly is as bright ivory overlaid with sapphires.
His legs are as pillars of marble,
 Set upon sockets of fine gold:…
His countenance is excellent …as the cedars.
His mouth is most sweet:
Yea, he is altogether lovely.
This is my beloved, and this is my friend."
   Song of Solomon 5:10-16

Passion

Driving Thoughts
The incredibly beautiful music in my ear
Brings my thoughts passionately to you.
Who are you – this man that haunts my dreams
And takes my thoughts on a rampage:
Running gaily through the meadow
When there is work to do?
I want you in my arms
And against my body.
I want to take your head in my hands –
My fingers long to run through your hair,
Grab a wad and pull gently until you squeak.
I dream of brushing my lips against your cheek
Searching for something more.
I discover your ears
And begin searching them with my tongue.

Upon Waking
My passion is a raging stallion.
Neighing wildly, it wants to run free, to mount.
Its eyes are glazed over a roaring fire –
Hot within.
Well the writer said, "It is better to marry
Than to burn."
I am burning, burning deep within.
Silence dampens the embers like ash.
Why do people want to put out my fire?
It is not good?
It is burning in a spirited being
Standing sentinel in an evening meadow
That has just escaped from a glowing sky.
Is it not beautiful? Should it not be free?

"My beloved spoke, and said to me,
Rise up, my love, my fair one, come away.
For, lo, the winter is past,
The rain is over and gone;
The flowers appear on the earth;
The time of the singing of birds is come,
And the voice of the turtle is heard in the land;
The fig tree puts forth her green figs,
And the vines with the tender grape give a good smell.
Arise, my love, my fair one, and come away.
O my dove, that bides in the clefts of the rock,
In the secret places of the stairs,
Let me see your sweet countenance,
Let me hear your voice;
For sweet is your voice,
And your countenance is comely...
My beloved is mine, and I am his.
He feeds among the lilies.
Until the day break, and the shadows flee away.
Turn, my beloved, and be like a roe or a young hart
On the mountains of Bether."

Song of Solomon 2: 10-17

Lenten Times

You say you are confused – uncertain.
You say you don't see clearly who you are
Or who you should spend your life with.
You say that your behavior toward me
That generated feelings of hurt was unintentional.
I believe you. What I am hearing is that you are unsure –
Of yourself – and unready for an intimate relationship.
I am sensing that you need some distance from me right now.
I am sure you can find some one else to accompany you
Where ever you want to go.
When you are ready to spend some time with me
And talk about how you feel and what you are thinking,
I am ready to see you again.
Lent is one of the best times for reevaluation
And spiritual insight.
It is this time of year when I turn my focus from worldly cares
And focus on something eternal.
Since you are a distraction from things internal and eternal,
I withdraw from you as well.
Warmth toward you is there as it has always been,
But there is no attachment.
You are like a butterfly – beautiful, fully alive,
And free to go where you will, stay in my garden,
Hover near or fly free.
I wish you joy.
I try to keep my personal feelings
Out of my decisions regarding people I care about.
(I am not always successful, as you may have noticed.)
You give me the freedom to express my need
When you do not accept responsibility for creating that need.
Thank you for being yourself.
I have needs that you may or may not be able to fill,
And you have needs that I may or may not be able to fill.
It is good to know that God supplies all our needs.
And whatever we do not have, we did not need.
We can trust Him fully.

Sunday Morning Reverie

The sparrows throw seed about as they titter
   on the birdfeeder.
Soft breezes stir the trees outside.
The early sun lights the garden, and
I sit quietly on the couch and wonder:
What do I want?
Who is he that shimmers, almost unseen,
On the edge of my dreams?
What does it mean:
The touch, the look, the kiss that I dream of?
What do I need?
And how will I recognize fulfillment
When I see it there before me?
I write an undelivered Note to the one I love:

What I want is the desire, expressed in positive ways,
To include me in your life.
What I am looking for is an interest in me as a person.
What I seek is your commitment to renew yourself
So that you know thoroughly that you are loved.
What I wait for is a positive invitation into your life –
Not just through a tiny peephole, but a conscious,
Physical and emotional revelation and sharing.
Open the peephole so I can see you more fully.
Share who you are with me in full daylight.
Face true intimacy with courage!
What I wonder about is the ways that you can bring
Joy and peace and pleasure into my life,
And I am alert for your actions revealing this plan.
You must win me. The game pieces are in place.
Tell me how you feel – with poetry
   (yours or someone else's),
Words, gifts, surprises, whatever.
Would you like to overcome your fears
And share this adventure called life with me?
I wait for you.

Earth's Mellow Comfort

Spring Flowering

Walking down a city street this April,
I am suddenly alerted to a delightful spring aroma,
And my thoughts turn to beauty and sweetness.
I know that there is a tree blooming
Somewhere in my vicinity,
And my heart rejoices.
A blooming tree has been well watered by autumn rains.

Occasionally those of us who live alone wonder
What benefit there is
In continuing our good deeds,
Keeping our minds focused, caring for ourselves,
And creating beautiful experiences
When there is no one special
In our lives to appreciate our accomplishments.
Sometimes I go for weeks
Without a comment from anyone
About my attractiveness, pleasant personality traits,
Cleverness, diligence, trustworthiness.
I sometimes wonder if anyone cares,
If anyone will ever care.
But now I see that just like a flowering tree,
Good deeds, careful work, creativity and attractiveness
Bring a pleasant experience to those who pass by –
Some too deeply embedded in their gloom to look up
And catch our glances.
And more than once, someone will stop to notice.
Just when we least expect it.
Courage grows. I am reassured:
I hear a voice saying,
"Do not weary in well doing."

"Your plants are an orchard of pomegranates
With pleasant fruits: camphire, with spikenard,
Spikenard and saffron; calamus and cinnamon,
With all trees of frankincense;
Myrrh and aloes, with all chief spices.
A fountain of gardens, a well of living waters,
And streams from Lebanon.
Awake, O north wind;
And come, thou south;
Blow upon my garden,
That the spices thereof may flow out.
Let my beloved come into his garden,
And eat his pleasant fruits."
Song of Solomon 4:12-16

"Trust in the Lord, and do good;
So shall you dwell in the land,
And truly, you will be fed.
Delight yourself also in the Lord,
And he shall give you the desires of your heart.
Commit your way unto the Lord;
Trust also in him;
And he shall bring it to pass...
Rest in the Lord, and wait patiently for him...
Cease from anger, and forsake wrath:
Do not fret yourself in any wise to do evil...
But the meek shall inherit the earth;
And shall delight themselves
In the abundance of peace...
Wait on the Lord and keep his way,
And he shall exalt you to inherit the land."
Selected verses from Psalm 37

Paradise

Beside the lake beneath Florida skies
I sense the vibrant growth of beauty around me.
The doves are cooing softly to their young
The gulls are crying to one another
About the sea! The sea!
Song birds are singing their sweet melody to the breeze,
And wood peckers are cleaning
The dead wood of hungry insects.
The sun's light is shining.
There is harmony in this lake's garden.

Except for my sneeze
And the raucous cawing of the blackbirds.
Everything is as it is.
Yesterday I discovered the hidden nest of a wood duck
Today the nest is disturbed
And the three softly rounded eggs are missing –
One lies unbroken on the shore of the lake.
Yesterday I saw the elegant plumage
Of the bird of paradise
Rise from a clump of harsh green swords.
Today I find the ugly brown dried remains
Of that thing of exciting beauty.
How many parts of life rise unexpectedly,
Burst into glorious flame
And dry to nothingness?

The majestic, exciting blossoms come and go
But the patient, inhospitable bush
Which gave birth to that glory lives on and on.
I cannot pick the glorious flower –
That would be an intrusion
On this paradise that is not mine.

But I can pick the withered flower stalk
To remind me of faded beauty.
The breeze and the sun rumple
The lake's surface revealing diamonds
Glittering on every tiny wave.
The ducks float and fish
Unaware of the glory that surrounds them.
A later visit to the nest reveals
A quiet mother intent on guarding her new eggs.

The sun warms my back,
And the singing birds warm my soul.
The aroma of the gardenia
Caresses the senses like
Smooth hands massage tight muscles.
The soft fragrance of plumaria
Coaxes peace and contentment
To awaken in the heart,
And I can be at peace in paradise.

"Let us get up early to the vineyards;
Let us see if the vine flourishes,
Whether the tender grape appears,
And the pomegranates bud forth:
There will I give thee my loves.
The mandrakes give a smell,
And at our gates
Are all manner of pleasant fruits,
New and old
Which I have laid up for thee,
O my beloved."
Song of Solomon 7:12-13

Birds in the Morning

What an amazing cacophony!
The ready voices of a dozen unseen birds
Call to one another in the early dawn.
And though their size and vocal apparatus
Is similar—their calls are all unique.
Even the timbre and tone of their voices are different.
The birds continue unabated.

For some, their song is a bright, lilting melody,
For some, their voice resembles
The continuing honk of a goose.
A few are repeating, "Tit, tit, tit,"
While caws from overhead break through at intervals.
Some have a message, repeated often,
Some in a deeper voice explain their cause.
They reinforce one another
And continue their rejoicing.
The raucous ones are interrupted
By the gentle soothing of a dove.

A cardinal performs a sensuous red wave
Against the background of the nearby meadow grass
And lands on the dry leaves, looking for breakfast.

The mellow greens of the forest entrance surround me,
And the bright rays of the rising sun
Bless me with holiness.
I am surrounded by beauty.
The gentle air comforts my body.
Even my ears are soothed with songs
From my winged friends.
This is what it means to be surrounded by love.
There is no fear in my soul.
I am refreshed.
And I discover again that I am the beloved.

*"Fair seed-time had my soul, and I grew up
Fostered alike by beauty and by fear; ...
When among the mountain-slopes
Frost, and the breath of frosty wind, had snapped
The last autumnal crocus, 'twas my joy
With store of springes o'er my shoulder hung
To range the open heights where woodcocks run
Among the smooth green turf. Through half the night, ...
Moon and stars were shining o'er my head. I was alone,
And seemed to be a trouble to the peace
That dwelt among them."*
— William Wordsworth

Earth's Comfort

Gently running stream,
Cascading over rocky barriers at my feet,
What do you have to teach me?
Three black birds shoot together from the glen at my right
Across the way, amongst the boulders
Bits of flowers brighten the landscape.
Tiny blue bells and violets
And strawberry flowers dot the ground beside me.

Three men – good men – three who do not know each other.
Three men – which of you is ready to know me?
Which, if any, desires closeness with me
Over freedom (as you see it)?
Or is there another in my future?
The sound of the running stream engages my mind,
Comforts my soul.
It flows clear and forever from an unseen source.
That is the way that nature produces beauty.
Mighty new trees growing from tiny pink sprouts
Smaller than a baby's finger.
That is how Nature supplies our unforeseen needs.
The oak begins to grow
Before the child is born who will climb it –
And see the future from its branches.
Endless sources, early planning, energy, purity,
Pleasant sounds and earthly beauty –
All these are intertwined so that Nature accomplishes goals
That the people it pleases have forgotten to request.
Thank God for creating a part of the world
Whose primary purpose seems to be to bring pleasure.
Blue skies filled with soft clouds,
The quiet droning of the early insects,
The continuous rush of the cold stream
Over earth bound stones,
The newest of flowers – fair shapes and colors
Framed in delicate green leaves
That were sheathed in pink buds last week –

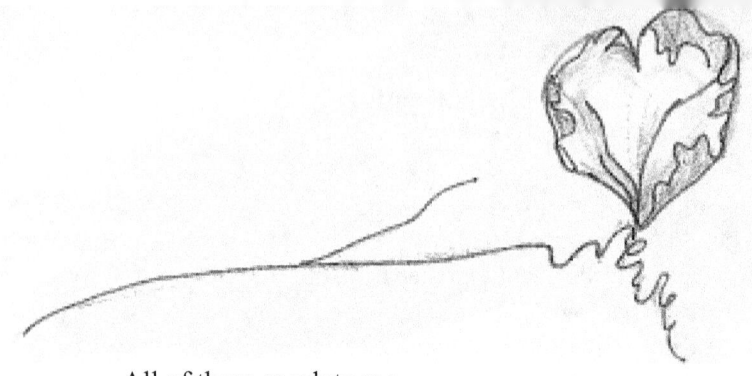

All of these speak to me
Of thoughtful purpose, perfection, planning
And prosperity beyond my understanding.
What more to I want
Besides someone to enjoy it with me?
Who will sit with me here, I wonder,
Enveloped in Nature's love,
Feeling the soft breeze and smelling
The gently turning earth rustling with new growth.
Who will it be?
And what season will he sit beside me on this crest?

A Valentine against the sky –
No, it is a browned leaf dried into beauty
With gentle curls of Nature's bidding.
He too, is a Valentine against the sky –
He is being prepared, even now,
To enjoy my beauty and softness.
He is being turned, as this gentle leaf, for my pleasure.
And I am being tuned for his.
There will come a day when
He and I will join Nature in its boundless revel.

> *"He shall be like a tree planted*
> *by the rivers of water, that brings forth fruit*
> *in his season; his leaf also shall not wither,*
> *and whatever he does*
> *shall prosper."*
> Psalm 1:3

"That twilight when we first begin to see
This dawning earth, to recognize, expect,
And, in the long probation that ensure,
The time of trial, ere we learn to live
In reconcilement with our stinted powers;
To endure this state of meager vassalage,
Unwilling to forgo, confess, submit,...
We know where we have friends."
— William Wordsworth

I Danced by the Sea
(sung to the rhythm of the sea)

I danced, danced, danced by the sea!

The sun appeared at the horizon
Casting its splendor across a wide sky.
The wind blew, chilling the viewer
Tossing my hair so that I could not see,

But I danced, danced, danced by the sea!

I wandered far, close by the sea foam.
I wandered out in the dry sand.
Searching and turning,
I sought several sea shells
(But brought only two black ones
    back to my friends)

While I danced, danced, danced by the sea!

The waves were crashing;
The birds were calling,
But I could not hear them,
    alone by the sea.
All those in the inn had white hair
    and someone.
I sat at my table alone drinking tea,

But I danced, danced, danced by the sea!

The wild birds were dipping,
    and screaming and skimming
Just inches above the blue beckoning waves.
The terns scattered safely all over the shoreline
Hunting in safety away from the waves

While I danced, danced, danced by the sea!

Crashing and playing at games of their own
The wild waves in harmony echo my song.
The music was there; the music sang sweetly.
I alone heart it; the music played on

As I danced, danced, danced by the sea!

Ah! The sea!
Ah! The dance!
When I arrive at home,
I'll tell Jack of
   my deep desire for dancing,
Or Tom,
Or one of the Jim's
   in my acquaintance.
Ah! I love
Dancing!